Tom,

Wishing a great guy and terrific professional the very best of success!

Warmest Wishes,

Ray Anthony

SKYROCKET YOUR SALES

SKYROCKET YOUR SALES

Ray Anthony

Author, Keynote Speaker,
Workshop Leader, Consultant

23 Skyland Place • The Woodlands, TX 77381
Phone: 281-364-7739   E-mail: Innovader@aol.com

PELICAN PUBLISHING COMPANY
GRETNA 1986

Library of Congress Cataloging-in-Publication Data

Slesinski, Raymond A.
  Skyrocket your sales.

  1. Selling—Psychological aspects. 2. Listening.
3. Questioning. 4. Nonverbal communication. I. Title.
HF5438.8.P75S55   1986   658.8'5   85-28452
ISBN 0-88289-485-4

Manufactured in the United States of America
Published by Pelican Publishing Company, Inc.
1101 Monroe Street, Gretna, Louisiana 70053

Contents

Preface

While researching this book, I interviewed salespeople, sales managers, and their customers—the people who buy retail and commercial/industrial products. One of the questions I asked them was this one: "What do you feel are the most important personal qualities that a salesperson should have?" Of customers specifically, I asked, "Describe the ideal salesperson that you would like to do business with."

Without getting into a lot of detail, I can say that this is the gist of the responses I got: "I think salespeople should be sincere, trustworthy, dependable, friendly, and caring." Many customers responded that they would like to deal with salespeople who "know their stuff about their product and their competitors," have "the ability and desire to fully understand my business environment and needs," and are "able to show me directly how their product or service can help me in my business." Finally, here is an answer from one conscientious buyer who summed it up nicely (and perhaps directly expressed what other customers were indirectly aiming to say): "I want to feel that a salesperson is working *with* me—kind of like a business partner who keeps my best interests in the forefront."

These statements from salespeople and customers reinforce the belief that selling is a very personal interaction between people. People affect people, and in order to be successful in a sales environment, it's necessary to develop strong interpersonal and communications skills. Demonstrating these skills will make it easier for a prospect to respect and like a salesperson. This book is intended to help the average salesperson understand and further develop his or her "people skills" and sales techniques in order to become more prospect-oriented. In this way, the potential buyer will view the salesperson as a decided asset to himself and his business. He will perceive the salesperson as a consultant or advisor who can help the prospect achieve his organizational and personal goals through the use of the salesperson's product or service.

My years of sales and sales training experience have shown me that a majority of salespeople need to improve their listening, questioning, and body language skills substantially. When I looked for a book to use in my training classes to cover these three areas in a meaningful way, I couldn't locate one. Because of my strong conviction that there is a great need for this information, I decided to write just such a book. It was written for salesmen and saleswomen who sell either products or services.

This book concentrates on three critical interpersonal communication skills: listening, body language, and questioning techniques. With these skills, a salesperson can become a problem-solver, can better establish rapport with his prospect, and can deal with all kinds of sales resistance in a more effective fashion. The sales benefits gained by developing these three skills are faster sales, greater sales, and easier, cleaner sales (fewer problems associated with the sale). The real bottom line is enhanced professionalism and image and greater job satisfaction. There are also many personal benefits.

This book was designed and written to represent real-life selling situations that salespeople encounter every day. It contains actual interpersonal communication and sales tools to use. For example, in the chapters on listening and questioning, there are a number of sample responses and completely worded questions for the reader to use in various selling situations. These valuable tools can be used immediately; they can benefit sales veterans as much as people who are new to selling. The book contains many other specific selling tips and techniques to use in responding to your prospect, thus ensuring positive and speedy movement toward your sale. I've used the term *buying* throughout, but it is a generic sales term that can also apply to any sales transaction—renting, leasing, or any agreement applying to the use of a product or service. The information about communication I've assembled is general enough to benefit everyone, not only salespeople, by improving interpersonal skills, thus improving a person's social and personal life as well as job performance.

To get the most out of this book, I recommend that you first read it through, then re-read the sections that you feel are most applicable and important to you in your selling and personal life. Please keep in mind that listening, interpreting body language, and questioning are skills to be learned and then developed into strong habits. This book will help you understand what skills you need to improve. The next step is up to you, and it's the most important one: practice, practice, practice!

Practice these interpersonal and communication skills every day—every time you're involved in a conversation. It's like developing any other skill or activity, e.g., learning how to play golf, operate a car, or fly a plane; you can't expect to be good at it by just reading a book about it. I improved my listening and other interpersonal skills after much effort, and I still have to improve and maintain proficiency in the areas that I've already developed. One of the hazards of writing a book and being a sales trainer is that you have a constant responsibility to be on your guard—to be a role model for the topics you've written about. And rightfully so! Being an "aural degenerate" is no way to impress your audience.

I have learned a great deal from writing this book and have truly enriched my life by improving my listening and other people skills. I hope that this book will help you achieve your goals and bring to you a greater measure of self-satisfaction. I wish you, the reader, the very best of success in your personal life and your sales career.

Acknowledgments

I'd like to acknowledge and express my appreciation to a number of very fine people. To Theresa Passabile, whose ideas, support, and love encouraged me to be creative. To Marianne Burnham for her very good initial editing assistance. To Charles Eusey for his legal assistance. To Michael Kokernak for his graphic art assistance. To Polly Theriot of Pelican Publishing for her interest, support, and excellent editing assistance throughout. To my parents, Tony and Toni, and my sister Theresa, who have always gently, patiently, and lovingly nurtured, supported, and motivated me to try to be the very best I can be and who taught me the great value of listening. And, finally, to all my friends who have been wonderfully supportive of all my endeavors. I am grateful to all of you. Thank you and God bless you all.

SKYROCKET YOUR SALES

1

Effective Listening

Effective listening is a rare skill possessed by few of us. It has often been called the missing link in communication because it is the least understood and researched and one of the most neglected parts of the communication process. S. I. Hayakawa, the renowned semanticist, said, "Listening is a relatively neglected subject. A good listener helps the speaker clarify—and often correct—his ideas in the course of expressing them. Children become good communicators if they have adults who are good listeners."

A Big Part of Your Day...

We listen all day long, usually without giving much thought to it, yet we do not often do it well. Given the importance of listening, as we'll see more vividly later on, it's clearly a skill worth developing, because the good listener is at a social and business advantage. William Ford Keefe, in his book *Listen Management!*, cites several studies that conclude that most executives spend between 45 percent and 63 percent of a workday listening; office managers can spend as much as 80 percent of their time focused on listening. Harold T. Smith of Brigham Young University recently conducted a business and industrial study to isolate critical managerial traits—the 20 percent portion of important qualities that yields 80 percent of all profits. Smith distributed a questionnaire to 457 members of the Academy of Certified Administrative Managers asking them to rank twenty traits or competencies in order of importance. Two of the top five competencies involved communication; listening was number one.

Formal research on listening probably got its start in 1926 when researcher Paul Rankin analyzed how people spent their non-sleeping time. He found out that we spend 70 percent of our time—7 minutes out of every 10—in some form of communication. The average breakdown of this time is shown in Illustration 1.

Even in follow-up studies done recently among representative cross-sections of the population (such as white- and blue-collar workers, college students, salespeople, or homemakers), the percentage breakdowns shown largely remained the same. Therefore, we can assume that on any workday, salespeople will typically spend 70-80 percent of their time in some form of communication, with listening the major activity.

The general benefits that anyone, regardless of occupation, can receive from listening are many. Here are just a few:

—Improved personal relationships with co-workers, bosses, friends, spouse, children, and relatives

—Enhanced, more professional image and personal prestige

—Better resolution of all types of conflicts; fewer misunderstandings, false expectations, and disappointments

—Improved performance in job interviews

—Greater effectiveness as an executive, manager, or administrator

—Ability to absorb new information faster and retain it longer

—Improved negotiating abilities

ILLUSTRATION 1
COMMUNICATION TIME ALLOTTED

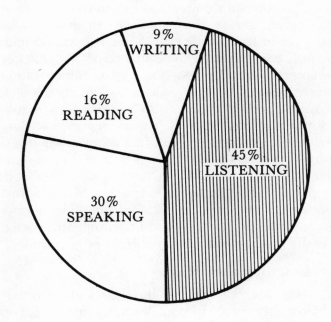

—Improved self-esteem

—Greater enjoyment of life

...But a Low-Priority Skill

Despite all the benefits of listening and the many costly problems poor listening can cause, few schools teach it, and only a few wise companies invest the time and money to train their employees to listen. Maybe the reason listening isn't widely taught is that our culture equates speaking ability with power and prestige. This is true to a large degree: a very good speaker can grab power and prestige from less dynamic individuals if speaking ability is the only consideration. As evidence of this, colleges and companies offer countless hours of seminar training to enhance presentation skills. Still, little or no time is allocated to formal listening training. As a result, few of us ever develop strong listening skills. The average person's listening effectiveness is only 25 percent. In a recent study conducted at a major university, tests given to 200 students showed that only 50 percent of oral information was retained immediately after being heard; after two months, the amount retained dropped to 25 percent. Since we need to listen in order to hold on to important information, we are really missing out on some great opportunities.

Poor Listening Can Hurt

So many problems in our business and personal lives can be directly traced to poor listening on our part or on the part of those we deal with. You order a scotch and soda in a bar and you get a scotch and water instead because the bartender wasn't listening. You go to pick up your car at the service station where you left it for some minor work and the mechanic hands you a bill for $225.76. You're shocked and angry, and you blurt out, "Just for a crummy transmission adjustment?" The mechanic, confused and defensive, counters with, "Adjustment? I thought you said transmission overhaul!" Or you tell your spouse to meet you at the small entrance to the shopping center in an hour, and he/she goes to the main entrance while you fume in another part of the mall.

These listening problems, though troublesome and annoying, are relatively minor. However, life and death situations can hinge on listening ability. For example, an airline pilot who is concentrating on his instrument readings and fails to listen carefully to air traffic controllers lands on runway 27 right instead of 27 left or climbs to 32,000 feet instead of the 36,000 feet specified. Either situation could result in a collision with other aircraft, resulting in a large loss of life. A nurse and a doctor who are not listening carefully to each other could administer the wrong medication or perhaps an unintentional overdose of the correct medication to a patient, which could be a fatal mistake. Poor listening has caused many lives to be lost in combat needlessly. A soldier walking through the jungle is surrounded by a myriad of natural sounds and does not hear the slight rustling of leaves caused by enemy soldiers preparing for an ambush, or even the unmistakable sound of one of those soldiers snapping back a rifle bolt to load his weapon.

Problems caused by poor listening have also been instrumental in causing divorces, ruining careers, severing friendships, and even starting wars. Misunderstandings, hurt feelings, and frustration could have been avoided (or at least minimized) by better listening. I'm convinced that many of the major problems resulting in the present Soviet-American deep freeze in diplomatic relations are caused by a lack of good listening. The two nations, with differing political ideals, past experiences, lifestyles, and values, refuse to make a sincere effort to truly understand each other, resolve differences, and change incorrect perceptions before they become major problems. To understand, each side must listen—openly, fairly, and sincerely. Understanding brought on by listening will improve the chances of compromise and agreement and, hence, better relations. We may not trust or like their government, and they may feel the same about us. However, in such a volatile, nuclear-weapons-saturated world, we really ought to put aside our mutual antagonisms and come up with a system that will allow us to live together, even if it's a delicate arrangement. Maybe the United Nations should resolve to teach all leaders, diplomats, and military personnel how to listen.

The business community also suffers large losses due to inadequate listening. The example often cited is that if each of America's approximately 105 million workers makes just one $10 mistake during the year, it adds up to over $1 billion a year. The mistakes could be as simple as having to retype a letter, shipping the wrong sales order, or announcing the wrong time for a meeting. Without having hard evidence for the cost of poor listening, I'd venture to say that it's really ten times that number—$10 billion—or maybe even way beyond that.

An article in the December 1984 issue of the *New Hampshire Business Review* cites another example of how costly listening mistakes can be. The article quotes Fritz Bell, founder of Walnut Hill Seminars in Raymond, New Hampshire, who teaches a course called "Improving Communication Through Listening." Bell gives this example of how seemingly minor individual listening mistakes add up to substantial waste over a period of time. A New England Telephone study showed that nearly 20 percent of its operator-assisted calls were delayed because of listening problems. The average delay was only 15 seconds, but when the company added up these wasted seconds over a period of a year, it came to an annual loss of $874,800. After the company began a program to teach effective listening, it reduced that amount by nearly $500,000.

For many companies, the average cost of just one sales call is over $100; the average cost of an industrial sales call has climbed to $205, according to McGraw-Hill Research. Suppose that, once a year, a salesperson didn't listen to the prospect about when to show up. The salesperson might have thought he heard 3 P.M. on Tuesday the 5th, but the prospect actually said 3 P.M. on Tuesday the 12th. The salesperson shows up on the 5th, and the prospect is not in. That's $100 down the tubes. If this happens to every salesperson in a company of 150 salespeople, you're talking about $15,000 lost— from just one listening mistake per year per salesperson. Salespeople and their managers know that listening problems and their related costs can be much, much higher than in this simple example. From my days in computer sales, I know of several big sales (over $200,000 each) lost by salespeople because they were somehow listening improperly. And I'm sure that I lost some sales, too, years ago when my listening skills needed sharpening.

The Bottom Line

What effect, then, can improved listening, questioning, and body language skills have on increased individual sales? And how much does that really translate into increased company revenues and profits? To help give insight into these issues, I conducted an informal survey of approximately 80 sales managers and salespeople selling various products for small to large companies in the Northeast. I suggested to each that there could be a way for the salespeople in his company to improve their listening, questioning, and body language reading skills so that their selling was improved in these ways:

—Better rapport with prospects, thus increasing the chances of getting follow-up meetings;

—Faster, more accurate qualifying skills;

—Better understanding of what the prospect needs and wants and how the prospect views the competition;

—Fewer misunderstandings and better ways to solve problems and personal conflicts;

—Improved sales presentations that focus better on what the prospect really needs and wants;

—More effective ways to handle objections; and

—Better reading of buying signals from the prospect that would result in quicker sales closes.

I then asked how much of an average percentage improvement did they think would result for all salespeople combined if these improvements were made. (As you read further, you'll understand how I arrived at the sales improvement benefits in the previous question.)

The answers that the sales managers and salespeople gave to this rather comprehensive question ranged from 5 percent to 80 percent. The average came out to approximately 20 percent improvement. Trying to measure sales increases that result from training—gaining new knowledge and skills—is extremely difficult to do, usually requiring costly, time-consuming scientific studies. So, just to illustrate the fact that listening, questioning, and body language training could have a very important dollar effect for a company, let's say that sales productivity will increase not by 20 percent, but a conservative 10 percent. Let's also assume that a company's pre-tax profit margin is 10 percent (revenues × 10%). Illustrations 2 and 3 show the projected increase in total company revenues (sales) and profits, respectively, based on the number of salespeople and the average sales quota per salesperson. By extrapolating from the figures shown, you can estimate the improvement in revenues and sales for your company that could result from improving the listening, questioning, and body language skills of your sales staff.

Let's take a look at one specific example to gauge the effect. Using the numbers in Illustration 2, suppose the average sales quota per salesperson selling commercial, industrial, or high-tech products or services is $500,000 per year (column 1). A 10 percent sales improvement will produce an extra $50,000 in increased sales for the company (column 2). Suppose a company has 100 salespeople, with the same average sales quota per salesperson. If all 100 increase their sales by an average of 10 percent, then total sales revenues for the company could increase by $5 million (column 3). Looking at Illustration 3, we see that this translates into $500,000 in increased company pre-tax profits (column 4).

This looks good on paper, of course, but should a company really go ahead and spend money to train its sales force in improved listening, questioning, and body language techniques? The next example should clearly answer that question. Let's be really conservative in our estimates this time. We'll use the same numbers we used in the previous example, except that we will now assume that an improvement in these skills only yields a 5 percent overall sales improvement per salesperson. Total company pre-tax profits would increase by "only" $250,000. Assuming that a results-oriented, high-quality two-day sales training course on listening, questioning, and body language costs $500 (excluding transportation, lodging, and other incidental costs) per salesperson (total costs: $50,000 for 100 salespeople), this comes out to a pre-tax simple return on investment of 500 percent ($250,000/$50,000). A negligible 1 percent improvement in sales as a result of training would be the break-even point on the investment. I think it's worth it.

ILLUSTRATION 2
INCREASED COMPANY REVENUES DUE TO IMPROVED
LISTENING, QUESTIONING, AND BODY LANGUAGE SKILLS

AVERAGE SALES QUOTA PER SALESPERSON	10% IMPROVEMENT IN SALES PER SALESPERSON	TOTAL COMPANY REVENUE INCREASE BY NUMBER OF SALESPEOPLE (MILLIONS OF DOLLARS) TOTAL NUMBER OF SALESPEOPLE IN COMPANY								
		25	50	100	200	300	400	500	750	1000
$ 100,000	$ 10,000	.25	.50	1	2	3	4	5	7.5	10
200,000	20,000	.50	1	2	4	6	8	10	15	20
500,000	50,000	1.25	2.5	5	10	15	20	25	37.5	50
750,000	75,000	1.87	3.75	7.5	15	22.5	30	37.5	56.25	75
1,000,000	100,000	2.5	5	10	20	30	40	50	75	100
1,500,000	150,000	3.75	7.5	15	30	45	60	75	112.5	150
2,000,000	200,000	5	10	20	40	60	80	100	150	200
2,500,000	250,000	6.25	12.5	25	50	75	100	125	187.5	250

ILLUSTRATION 3
INCREASED COMPANY PROFITS DUE TO IMPROVED
LISTENING, QUESTIONING, AND BODY LANGUAGE SKILLS

AVERAGE SALES QUOTA PER SALESPERSON	TOTAL COMPANY PROFIT INCREASE BY NUMBER OF SALESPEOPLE (MILLIONS OF DOLLARS)								
	TOTAL NUMBER OF SALESPEOPLE IN COMPANY								
	25	50	100	200	300	400	500	750	1000
$ 100,000	.025	.05	.10	.20	.30	.40	.50	.75	1.0
200,000	.05	.10	.20	.40	.60	.80	1.0	1.5	2.0
500,000	.125	.25	.50	1.0	1.5	2.0	2.5	3.75	5.0
750,000	.187	.375	.75	1.5	2.25	3.0	3.75	5.62	7.5
1,000,000	.25	.50	1.0	2.0	3.0	4.0	5.0	7.5	10
1,500,000	.375	.75	1.5	3.0	4.5	6.0	7.5	11.25	15
2,000,000	.50	1.0	2.0	4.0	6.0	8.0	10	15	20
2,500,000	.625	1.25	2.5	5.0	7.5	10	12.5	18.75	25

This book, like any quality course on improving listening, questioning, and body language, will only yield results when the salesperson continually uses and fine-tunes the skills learned. Studies have shown that salespeople lose as much as 70-90 percent of the value of a book or training seminar if they never use what they've learned.

A Success Story

Today's companies usually recognize the fact that buyers are more sophisticated, educated and knowledgeable about products now than ever before. The old way to sell—to tell—is out; the new way—to act as a business consultant to the prospect—is in. And listening plays a key role in that important transition. So more and more companies are getting on the listening bandwagon to make their salespeople and other employees more productive. Senior-level managers, especially, tend to insulate themselves (intentionally or not) from the line personnel in their company, even though these workers often have excellent ideas to improve the company's operation or perhaps have legitimate gripes that are adversely affecting their productivity and morale. Listening training has had its share of powerful endorsers such as Westinghouse, General Motors, U.S. Steel, American Telephone and Telegraph, Western Electric, and Dow Chemical Company. But the company that is always referred to as an example of what good listening training can do for employees is Sperry, the computer manufacturer.

For Sperry, it started several years ago with the slogan, "It all begins with listening." From the start, the advertising messages concentrated not on how well Sperry listened, but on how important it was for almost everyone to develop effective listening skills. The subtle, indirect message was that Sperry people will listen to you, the customer. And they *did* listen, because they cared and they were trained to. Sperry executives realized how a good listener sparkles among the rest like a fine gem.

Sperry's chairman and chief executive at the time, J. Paul Lyet, had asked his advertising and public relations executives to find a solid, meaningful theme that would have a strong and lasting effect on the public, enhance the image of Sperry, and help distinguish it from other computer companies, just as the slogan and philosophy "We try harder" had done for Avis Rent-A-Car. Sperry contacted Dr. Lyman K. Steil, a listening expert at the University of Minnesota, and Dr. Steil developed an effective one-day listening program. When the campaign and training were launched in 1979, the reaction and results were far greater than most people had anticipated.

Although it started as just another publicity campaign, listening took on an almost religious importance at Sperry. It became an everyday part of business. Listening was instrumental in helping Sperry make the needed transition from an engineering, high-technology-oriented company to one that now translates high-quality products and services into customer solutions—a high-quality marketing company.

Sperry's listening program trained approximately 15,000 people worldwide in various job positions and categories. One of the reasons that it was an unqualified success was that it received high-level support from the corporation's senior executives, who also attended the training course. In addition to creating a "Sperry identity" in the industry, listening training did positively affect the quality of operations throughout the company.

How did listening positively impact Sperry's employees? First of all, people left the listening course with a greater awareness of the need to improve their listening techniques. However, before the course, many of the people were skeptical of its value. They wondered why the company was spending money on what was originally perceived as a conceptual-type course that covered a subject (listening) that was originally thought to be rather basic and common-sense in nature. Many wondered why a more practical job-related course (e.g., something product-related) was not chosen. A majority of the participants had a distinct positive change in attitude toward listening. Approximately 45 percent actually underwent a change in behavior that made them more sensitive and responsive to "human issues" and, therefore, more productive in the areas of identifying and solving business needs—specifically market-related problems.

In general, those participating felt that the listening seminar enabled them to have more control over their actions, and they felt that it gave them strong interpersonal tools to better handle hostile, antagonistic situations with both customers and co-workers. In addition, managers felt an enhanced ability to motivate their staffs. An important auxiliary benefit of the listening training was that participants felt that their domestic and personal lives were improved as a result of becoming better listeners. The initial skepticism and apathy that employees had when the listening campaign was started quickly turned and blossomed into a rush of other employees who wanted to undergo the training. Even Sperry's customers wanted to find out more about this "passion for listening" that Sperry was touting. They wanted to train their own people; they wanted to get hooked on listening.

For every company that recognizes the value of instilling good listening habits in its employees, there are hundreds of others that have not yet accepted the listening value factor, or agree that listening is important but refuse to take the vital step to fund a good, results-oriented training program. Unfortunately, too many top executives don't see it as an investment in their company's future. As an example, the aforementioned Dr. Steil relates the following story, which appeared in an article in the May 26, 1980, *U.S. News and World Report.*

On an airplane trip, Dr. Steil talked with the president of a small company and asked him if his firm had experienced any problems because of his employees' inability or failure to listen. Apparently the question struck a nerve, because according to Dr. Steil, the man's eyebrows went up, and he told how his company had recently lost a million-dollar sale. "Two of my employees were involved," the executive said. "One didn't hear the important message at all, and the other one misinterpreted it. The upshot was that we lost out on a bid that we should have won hands down." Dr. Steil asked, "Knowing that you lost a million-dollar order as a result of poor listening, would you be willing to spend, say, $100,000 over a period of time to develop your employees' listening ability?" The response was typical: "I'm not sure."

If the listening training at Sperry was so well advertised and so well received by its employees, why haven't many other companies begun to institute listening programs (even modest ones) on a trial basis? The answer is that listening still has the unwarranted stigma of being a passive type of personal activity—as opposed to more practical training that would allegedly impact a company's bottom line more effectively. Obviously Sperry felt different about instituting a large listening program, and so did its satisfied customers—a worthwhile investment indeed.

The remarkably successful business book *In Search Of Excellence* and its sequel, *A Passion For Excellence,* stress the crucial need for a company to constantly think in terms of pleasing its customers and innovate in order to stay at the top of the market. Concern, dedication, and an almost religious crusade to do things right, produce superior products, and deliver outstanding service are the underlying "excellence" themes of both books. The books suggest that the major managerial productivity problem in America stems from managers being out of touch with their customers and insulated from people in their own organizations. Sitting pretty in the isolated ivory towers of big business has taken its toll for companies in every industry.

In *A Passion For Excellence,* authors Tom Peters and Nancy Austin talk about the importance of listening. They strongly recommend "naive listening"—listening to the people whom you ultimately affect directly (your customers) and not just other people who are in the marketing chain, yet are farther removed from the real, day-to-day experiences that you need to know about. Naive listening means getting information "right from the horse's mouth," without the risk of distortion from going through intermediaries. This type of listening to customers and employees is critical for successful companies because a major share of new ideas and directions come from these important people. Raw, direct listening that keeps company officers quickly and accurately tuned into key, "gut" concerns that customers and caring employees have is needed—concerns that can prevent a firm's collapse or slow, painful death; concerns that can catapult an organization to the top and keep it there (if its leaders continue to listen and correctly respond to their customers).

In a recent meeting with a group of managers, Philip Caldwell, former chairman of the Ford Motor Company, talked about a program at Ford called Employee Involvement. It recognizes that everyone in Ford has something worthwhile to contribute and, therefore, it's vital to listen to each person's ideas. He said, "You see, if we don't care enough to create the climate and we don't care enough to ask somebody, and if we don't care enough to listen to what people tell us, then we won't engender the attitude that results in suggestions and participation."

Effective leaders who carefully listen to their employees are sure of the results of good listening. Spouses who strive to listen to their partners are sure of the relationship rewards of developing good listening habits. And, finally, successful salespeople—those who not only make sales quotas, but even break records year after year—are sure of the immense benefits of listening to their prospects and established customers.

Hearing Versus Listening

"Yeah, I hear what you're saying." How many times has someone told you that? In moments of anger, frustration, or tension you might have replied, "I know you've heard me, but have you listened to what I've said?" There is a big difference between hearing and listening. Hearing is the physical occurrence whereby sounds are registered in a person's ear. Hearing does not require any effort. People are aware of sounds around them and usually become so accustomed to them that they become oblivious to them. During each day we hear a multitude of sounds at once. In an office environment, for example, you may hear conversations around you, typewriters clicking away, phones ringing, people walking nearby, and perhaps outside street noises all being aimed at you.

I lived in Queens, New York City, near JFK Airport for over 30 years, and I became accustomed to hearing typical city noises at night before I went to sleep—noises such as traffic, sirens, and especially low-flying airplanes. When I moved to Merrimack, a relatively small town in New Hampshire, I had difficulty sleeping at first because of the total silence of the rural, relatively isolated area. I just wasn't used to it. To me, long accustomed to hearing and ignoring all the sounds of the busy city, the silence was deafening. The same thing often happens to a husband or wife (or both) after a number of years of marriage. After five, ten, or fifteen years, one partner physically hears the other talking but, like any other surrounding sound, tunes it out—listening to the television instead, concentrating on reading a paper or magazine, daydreaming, or thinking about what to say next. Years ago as excited lovers they would have clung to and soaked up each other's every word, never breaking intense eye contact. "Listening atrophy" interferes with communication. It is a major reason why personal relationships are so often dissolved, both emotionally and legally.

Listening is a learned skill that is worlds apart from hearing. Listening is hearing with a purpose. It is a highly active process in which a person pays careful attention by concentrating on what a speaker is saying. We hear many sounds, but we selectively listen for specific sounds. And in personal conversations we listen for meanings and overall messages, ideas, and feelings. Listening, then, requires attention, thought, and concentration to arrive at an outcome. Illustration 4 sums up the major differences between hearing and listening.

When we listen effectively, we are digesting, synthesizing, analyzing, and interpreting what is and is not being said. Good listening means getting an accurate, complete understanding of what a speaker means. It's not just listening for facts, but figuring out the sum total of all the facts, weighing the facts against each other, and making associations that will help us decipher the message being communicated. That's meaningful listening.

Effective listening is also selective listening, when called for. A good automobile mechanic, for example, can listen to an engine to isolate certain sounds indicating a specific problem. The mechanic analyzes the noise to determine if the car engine is knocking, a valve lifter is defective, a piston is slapping against the cylinder wall because of a broken piston ring, or any other problems exist. A cardiologist carefully listens to a person's heartbeat with a

ILLUSTRATION 4
HEARING VS. LISTENING

HEARING...	LISTENING...
is a purely physical function	is a mental and emotional experience (uses logic and feelings)
is a simple activity (you just hear sounds)	is a complex activity (requires analysis, interpretation, translation)
is automatic; doesn't take effort	requires dedicated effort— attention and long-term concentration
is a natural function (unless hearing is impaired)	is a learned skill
can take in all sounds combined	isolates sounds, looks for specific meanings and ideas
is easy	can be difficult and tiring
everyone who can, hears	few people are excellent listeners
is a prerequisite for listening, but otherwise has no intrinsic value to it	is usually done for selfish reasons (listener enjoys what's being said or gets valuable information from it)
	yields personal and career benefits

stethoscope to detect abnormalities in strength and rhythm or other factors. The doctor hears a number of sounds, but he listens specifically for certain sounds or their absence. A music expert can listen to and savor the sound of each instrument in an orchestra, however subtle the sound may be. This same music lover probably would not pay much attention to the piped-in music that we hear in banks, department stores, shopping malls, and restaurants. That's selective listening.

Active listening is a valuable way to listen, because the listener focuses not only on what is being said, but also on how it is being said (pauses, tone of voice, slight hesitation, body language, and other factors). Active listening reveals to the sensitive listener more than words alone. When a person uses active listening—listens with his ears *and* eyes—he can respond appropriately to the speaker. The improved ability to respond makes the listener able to say honestly, "I understand what you've said." Active listening tells a speaker that you care enough to display your interest in what he or she thinks and feels. This type of listening makes personal conversations more relaxed, fluid, and on track—hence, more effective. It draws relationships together, cementing interpersonal bonds quickly. That's active listening.

When people feel that you not only understand them but eagerly want to continue to work at understanding them and perhaps even help them, they are drawn to you. They are attracted like a magnet because of your caring, sincerity, and human warmth. How many people go out of their way to make you feel special—to put you at the forefront of the conversation by listening and responding in a supportive fashion to your opinions and feelings? Probably not enough, right? It's a great feeling when someone does. We fragile human beings love to be loved; we like to be "stroked," to get respect, to know that others truly care. Those special people who do care use magnetic listening.

Because listening is a complex process requiring concentration and effort, it's not an easy activity to do for long periods of time. However, with practice, it becomes easier. For example, college students sitting in on an important but hard to understand lecture that they will be tested on immediately afterwards can become exhausted after only 45 minutes of strenuous listening. The very process of extended, strenuous listening for a number of hours has been reputed to burn up several hundred calories!

Try substituting the word *listening* for *hearing* when alerting someone to the fact that you are, indeed, paying attention. See what a difference it makes in dealing with your prospects, friends, spouse, or co-workers. For example, instead of saying "I hear what you're saying," say "I'm carefully listening to you."

Effects on the Selling Process

Effective listening and questioning techniques and understanding body language are the essential elements of a strong foundation in any sales endeavor. While these skills are especially important to use in the beginning of the sales cycle to get valuable information needed for the sale, they are also used throughout the selling process. Illustration 5 shows a simplified but valid sales process model that includes the proper sequence of sales steps to perform. Selling involves clearly and completely identifying what a prospect needs and wants and then explaining to him in a believable way how your product or service can best meet those needs and wants. Listening and questioning are the burrowing tools you need to do this.

Let's take a deeper look at the selling process shown in the model. In Step 1, the salesperson is in an information-

ILLUSTRATION 5
SALES PROCESS MODEL

ELEMENTS OF THE SALES STEPS

TYPICAL SEQUENTIAL
STEPS IN SELLING

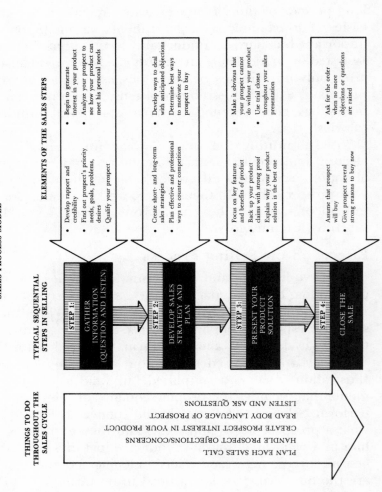

STEP 1:
GATHER INFORMATION (QUESTION AND LISTEN)

- Develop rapport and credibility
- Find out prospect's priority needs, goals, problems, desires
- Qualify your prospect

- Begin to generate interest in your product
- Analyze your prospect to see how your product can meet his personal needs

STEP 2:
DEVELOP SALES STRATEGY AND PLAN

- Create short- and long-term sales strategies
- Plan effective and professional ways to counter competition

- Develop ways to deal with anticipated objections
- Determine best ways to motivate your prospect to buy

STEP 3:
PRESENT YOUR PRODUCT SOLUTION

- Focus on key features and benefits of product
- Back up your product claims with strong proof
- Explain why your product solution is the best one

- Make it obvious that your prospect cannot do without your product
- Use trial closes throughout your sales presentation

STEP 4:
CLOSE THE SALE

- Assume that prospect will buy
- Give prospect several strong reasons to buy now

- Ask for the order when no more objections or questions are raised

THINGS TO DO THROUGHOUT THE SALES CYCLE

PLAN EACH SALES CALL
HANDLE PROSPECT OBJECTIONS/CONCERNS
CREATE PROSPECT INTEREST IN YOUR PRODUCT
READ BODY LANGUAGE OF PROSPECT
LISTEN AND ASK QUESTIONS

gathering role, using concentrated listening and questioning to get the necessary data. A professional *never* begins a sales call with a sales pitch; that's tellin', not sellin', and it establishes an unproductive one-way conversation. The professional creates an equal dialogue by listening and questioning to find out how he can help the prospect achieve his goals, meet his needs, solve his problems, or fulfill his aspirations through the salesperson's product or service. Although being articulate and convincing is a valuable personal sales asset, a successful salesperson isn't just a smooth talker, but an excellent listener, too. During Step 1 in the sales process, the salesperson also uses questions and listens to qualify the prospect—that is, to determine if the prospect has the authority, funds, need, and willingness to purchase the product. If not, the salesperson is wasting his time. (A more detailed explanation of qualifying can be found in chapter 7.) Good salespeople know what information they need and go after it.

The salesperson with his need to gather information prior to giving a product-oriented solution to the prospect is very much like a doctor or news reporter. Like a doctor, for example, the salesperson is out to cure the prospect's ills by prescribing his product or service. A doctor usually doesn't recommend a corrective cure before diagnosing exactly what the physical problem is. He needs information and can't afford to take a rough guess at what's ailing the patient. So in the beginning, when a doctor first sees a patient, he asks questions and listens—questions like, "Exactly where does it hurt?" "What type of pain are you having? What does the pain feel like—a sharp, stabbing pain in a specific spot, or a blunt pain that's spread out?" "How often do you have the pain and how long does it usually last?" Then the doctor takes appropriate diagnostic tests to get at the source of the problem.

Highly skilled (and highly paid) news reporters are successful because they are consummate questioners and excellent listeners who get people to open up quickly. Consider Barbara Walters. She has a distinctive ability to get personal with famous and powerful people, even people who have the reputation of being unapproachable, tight-lipped, or defensive. She quickly disarms the celebrity and creates a relaxed, non-intimidating environment for her subject to share personal feelings and secrets with millions of television viewers. Her successful interviewing technique is heavily dependent on good listening, pointed questions, a soft voice combined with frequent smiles, and her reading of and reacting to a person's body language.

In Step 2 of our sales process model, the salesperson develops short- and long-term strategies to continue the sale in a positive direction. This includes creating ongoing plans that tell him what other prospects he should see, when to see them, what areas to discuss during the sales call, and, most important, what objectives to accomplish during the sales call. These strategies and tactics may have to be updated and modified as conditions change.

Step 3, presenting a solution, occurs only after the salesperson has pieced together a complete and accurate picture of the prospect's needs, problems, and goals. Following his sales strategy, he then proceeds to give a carefully prepared, convincing, and relevant sales presentation that focuses on the solution that his product or service can offer. He focuses exclusively on those product features and benefits that directly relate to the prospect's needs or problems. He avoids the canned presentations that some salespeople use as a forum to spout about any and all irrelevant features connected with their product. During his presentation, the effective salesperson carefully watches the prospect's body language to gauge his reaction to the presentation and then dynamically adjusts the presentation accordingly to get the sale.

Professional salespeople never sell their product or service during the sales presentation. They sell solutions that their products provide for the prospect; they sell the value of their products; and they create profitable or otherwise satisfying business and personal opportunities for the prospect through their products. In some situations with some select products, a creative, well-meaning salesperson can make dreams come true for his prospects. As an example, cosmetic salespeople are taught not to just sell cosmetics, but to sell the beauty, illusion of youth, and sexiness that can result from using them. A good salesperson always wants to create and maintain his prospect's interest in his product by pointing out important and beneficial aspects of the product as early as possible and throughout the sale. But he never begins a complete sales presentation until he uncovers all the important needs, requirements, and wants of his prospect, and only then does he build his organized and persuasive presentation around them.

Finally, in Step 4 of the sales process model, the salesperson subtly and ever so effectively closes the sale. The close should be made only after the salesperson has specifically presented how the product or service will benefit the prospect. However, he should close the sale whenever the prospect has apparently made his mind up to buy, even if this happens before the salesperson goes into a presentation. Books about selling written ten to twenty years ago tell the salesperson to begin closing the sale the moment he meets the prospect—to actually ask closing questions without having the slightest idea what the prospect needs and wants. That's coming on way too strong, and I'm sure you and I don't like the hard sell with some anxious salesperson breathing down our necks. That's pushing, not guiding; that's tellin', not sellin'.

Today, many salespeople still think that closing the sale is the toughest and roughest part of selling. That's where they believe they have to brace themselves to do battle with the prospect in a kind of contest or struggle to see who has the strongest willpower. Some see getting the sale as a win-lose situation. The professional, on the other hand, sees it otherwise; he sees it as a win-win opportunity for himself and the prospect. The close of a sale will be the easiest part of selling if Steps 1-3 in the sales process model are performed properly. This is because all a salesperson is essentially doing is helping the prospect discover and understand exactly how the product or service being sold can meet his important needs and wants. If a salesperson executes Steps 1-3 in a proficient way, the prospect will then be self-motivated to buy.

The salesperson using this philosophy and selling model quickly rises above the status of peddler and takes on the important and prestigious role of business consultant, advisor, problem-solver—a decided asset to the prospect. And that not only translates into one sale now, but also greatly helps to establish a good, solid personal and business relationship that will lead to other ongoing sales in the future.

There's actually another important step after the close, and that's supporting your prospect (post-sale support); this differs from hit-and-run selling. The trend toward long-term account management for many vendors means that servicing customers after the sale is just as critical as the attention focused on the prospect prior to getting a sales contract. Listening, questioning, and body language skills play an important part after the sale. If a customer has a question or concern about his product or service, he wants to know that the salesperson is there to help. Good post-sale support can only help to secure future sales from that prospect. And good service means listening to customers at all times. Selling with post-sale support is almost like a marriage—you shouldn't stop acting your best simply because a legal contract was signed.

While the close is much easier for the consultant type of salesperson, there will still often be obstacles and objections to handle from the prospect. But a seasoned, polished sales professional weathers those situations by alert, caring listening and questioning and by maintaining a friendly attitude of interest and understanding. This encourages the prospect to open up, to discuss any concerns intelligently and calmly, and to facilitate a mutual agreement that leads to the sale. With proper listening and questioning, the salesperson never has to push, intimidate, or use other clever tricks to squeeze a sale from the prospect. He simply attempts to provide satisfactory answers to help the prospect arrive at his own conclusion—to discover for himself that he should purchase the product or service.

What I have described here is not passive selling. On the contrary, this is a very powerful way to sell, because it directs all of a salesperson's energy toward getting a prospect to recognize needs that a salesperson's product can fill and then giving very justifiable reasons to buy the product, without ever putting external pressure on the prospect. There is a tremendous amount of pressure on the prospect, but it's internal (self-motivating) pressure to buy, because the salesperson has suggested new and vital opportunities to consider regarding the product. In this way, the prospect never feels he was sold something. Instead, he feels that he bought the product based on his own desires and decision. And the prospect will trust, like, and respect the salesperson for helping to supply information and guidance without coercion, sales tricks, or other clever forms of manipulation or pressure. The prospect will be highly inclined to buy from that salesperson again and again.

Selling using the four steps outlined in the sales process model is like building a solid pyramid. The strong foundation is determining and then addressing through your product the needs, objectives, or problems of the prospect. The capstone or tip of the pyramid, the last piece to be put into place, is the close. When a salesperson starts off the sales process with a sales pitch and tries to close the sale before he has built up a stable foundation of personal rapport, professional credibility, answers, and solutions for the prospect, he is attempting to build a pyramid upside down.

To sum up, a sale is immensely easier when a salesperson uses good listening and questioning and can read body language signals throughout the sales cycle. By keeping the amount of your talking down (especially in the beginning) and asking meaningful questions, you will guide the prospect efficiently, yet gently, from initial contact toward grateful involvement with your product or service.

How Good a Listener Are You?

Have you ever evaluated your listening habits or those of others? If not, the following quiz will give you some initial insights into your present listening ability. Like many quizzes, it's easy to figure out which answers will give you a higher score, but to get the most out of the evaluation, be completely objective and honest with yourself. If you've taken other listening tests before, this might serve as a useful second evaluation. If this is your first listening test, keep in mind that the score you receive is designed to give you a general view of your present listening status. Chapter 4 will give you specific suggestions on how to improve your listening.

If you're really daring, you may want to ask your friends, co-workers, and (especially) your spouse to fill out the test on you to see how they perceive your listening habits. In this way, you can get several opinions to help you really assess your present listening skills. You may be surprised at the results!

Listening Test

Using the scoring system below, put a check mark in the appropriate column for each question. Then add up your points to arrive at a total score and see which listening category you fall into.

Answer	*Points*
Almost always	*5*
Often	*4*
Occasionally	*3*
Seldom	*2*
Practically never	*0*

In your conversations with people, do you...	**Almst Alwys**	**Often**	**Occly**	**Sldom**	**Prac Nver**
SCORE ..	5	4	3	2	0
1. Tend to interrupt the other person?					
2. Finish the other person's sentences, even when he/she is not groping for words?					
3. Tend to daydream and let your mind wander?					

	5	4	3	2	0
4. Automatically assume that you know what the other person will say before he/she says it?..					
5. Immediately jump into a conversation the moment that the person speaking pauses to take a breath?..............					
6. Try to write down practically everything the speaker says in taking notes?					
7. Abruptly change the subject before the speaker has had an adequate opportunity to make a point?......					
8. Find yourself doing most of the talking during a typical sales call?					
9. Attempt to be witty or flippant when the speaker appears to have something serious to discuss?...........					
10. Pretend to listen just to be polite or because the speaker would get angry if he/she caught you not listening?					

	5	4	3	2	0
11. Let distractions such as noise, outside activity, or room decor prevent you from concentrating on what the speaker is saying?					
12. Find it very difficult to have an open mind toward new ideas and ways of doing things? . .					
13. Appear to rush the speaker because you are pressed for time and want the speaker to get straight to the point?					
14. Let your emotions strongly affect your listening when the speaker talks about something controversial or painful to hear? . . .					
15. Avoid smiling, nodding, or using terms like *uh-huh* while you are listening?					
16. Hear only those things you want to hear and reject all else?					

	5	4	3	2	0
17. "Turn off" to a speaker because of personality, voice mannerisms, age, sex, or appearance?					
18. Find yourself jumping to hasty conclusions before getting sufficient information?					
19. Keep silent if you aren't completely sure you understand the speaker instead of clarifying what you think you heard?					
20. Go ahead with what you are doing rather than giving the speaker your full, undivided attention? ...					
21. Strongly prefer that people not talk about themselves, but instead concentrate on you and what you are saying?					
22. Just focus on details rather than trying to understand the overall message that the speaker is trying to convey?					

	5	4	3	2	0
23. Ignore a speaker's body language and tone of voice?					
24. Sense that most people avoid seeking your advice on personal or otherwise sensitive subjects?					
25. Avoid listening to complex or boring (but potentially important) information?					
26. Look at people in an evaluative, judgmental, or otherwise critical way when they speak?					
27. Fiddle with objects (pens, paper clips, cups) or exhibit other distracting mannerisms while listening?					
28. Sense that most people get frustrated at you for some reason?					
29. Ask the speaker questions that indicate you aren't fully listening?.					

	5	4	3	2	0
30. Repeatedly look at your watch while listening to someone?					

TOTAL SCORE...................... _____

What Your Score Means

10-49	Excellent listener
50-69	Good listener
70-99	Average listener
100-119	Poor listener
120-150	Major listening problems

2

Purposes and Benefits of Listening

A good listener is not only popular everywhere,
but after a while he knows something.

WILSON MIZNER

Developing strong, effective listening skills can have a dramatic impact on a salesperson's success. Often the benefits of good listening can be realized within a short period of time. The important thing about listening is that it applies to *all* types of selling, from relatively simple retail items to sophisticated, long-term selling of high-tech products and services.

Apart from the business benefits received from listening, there are many spinoff benefits that strengthen personal relationships between spouses, friends, and relatives. Here are the major reasons and benefits of effective listening:

- Helps the salesperson quickly develop and maintain rapport with a prospect
- Enables a salesperson to obtain vital information needed for the sale
- Makes selling easier for the salesperson
- Improves the salesperson's professional image
- Defuses tense situations
- Is persuasive

35

Developing Rapport with a Prospect

Developing a lasting rapport with your prospect quickly is critical in getting a sale and establishing a long-term relationship with an organization. Rapport is defined as a close relationship, usually one of mutual trust and emotional harmony. Good listening can do wonders to build trust and friendship in any social situation. Listening is a strong interpersonal skill that should be used on the very first sales call and continued throughout the sales process.

Given a choice, prospects will always buy from people they like. One of the few times a person will buy something from a salesperson that he doesn't like or trust is when that salesperson is selling a product or service that nobody else has and that the prospect desperately needs. Another time is when the prospect can get such an irresistible discount that it warrants dealing with that salesperson temporarily.

Prospects are more prone to do favors for salespeople they like. It's an accepted fact of life: we do favors for friends and other people we like that go beyond what we normally do for others. Because good listening fosters rapport and solidifies friendship, a prospect who likes you is:

—Less likely to be resistant to your ideas, recommendations, and proposals

—More apt to do things for you than he would for your competitors (for example, arranging an important appointment for you to meet with his boss to discuss your sales proposal or agreeing to visit your manufacturing plant to see a quality-control demonstration despite his busy schedule)

—More willing to give you exclusive information to help in your sale (information that is normally privy only to select people in the organization)

—More apt to get involved in your sales proposal and perhaps help you sell it to others in the organization

The trend in many organizations' sales forces is toward large account selling—the Fortune 2000 accounts. The goal is to establish a profitable, stable ongoing business relationship with an account so that a salesperson can increase his business continually and provide follow-up support after the sale. You cannot attain this result without developing rapport with the key decision-makers in the account.

Listening on the part of the salesperson makes a prospect feel he is in control and can do exactly as he wishes. Prospects equate a salesperson in a constant talk mode with being sold. They feel that the salesperson is trying to overwhelm them with persuasive rhetoric that may entice them into a hasty decision that they will later regret.

The following are some ways in which listening establishes rapport with a person.

Listening is tremendously complimentary to your prospect. When someone sincerely listens to us, it's one of the highest forms of acknowledgment and appreciation we can be shown. A good listener is a silent flatterer. He or she makes us feel intelligent, important, and respected. When a person listens, he acknowledges us by indirectly but strongly saying, "You, your opinions, and your feelings are important to me." A receptive listener can increase the self-esteem of the speaker, which is a basic, universal human need.

Talking to a good listener is enjoyable. It's a lot easier for salespeople who are good listeners to get repeat appointments to see their prospects, because their good listening skills make them enjoyable to be with, in addition to it being good business. Many salespeople make it a regular practice to orient their conversations toward the prospect. They ask the prospect questions, then sit back and listen intently. The result is a "superglue" type of rapport that cements a good relationship between prospect and salesperson. Asking a prospect the following types of questions enables a salesperson to begin an enjoyable (and most likely productive) conversation:

> "How did you get started in this fascinating business?"
>
> "I'd like to hear more about your ideas on expanding your business. Besides my being fascinated with it, I believe our company can substantially help you in that goal."
>
> "I read that article about you in *Business Week*. That project of yours has got to be a smashing success. How did you get the idea to implement this concept before anyone else in the whole industry?"

People don't have time to listen to salespeople who rave on and on about their products. Prospects are, however, very willing to spend time with someone who is interested in their needs, problems, ideas, and feelings. Salespeople like that are sure to get welcomed back by the prospect every time. Benjamin Disraeli said, "Talk to a man about himself and he will listen for hours." It's true. As a salesperson, I no longer worry about trying to impress my prospects by being a smooth, interesting speaker. I do emphasize dynamic speaking skills in group presentations, but in the company of one or two prospects, I try to be a good listener. The shortcut to popularity is to use your ears, not your tongue. My friend David Hodges, a professor at Hunter College in New York, is a naturally great listener. When someone talks to him, his whole body seems to listen, absorbing every word. He's quick to laugh at your jokes, compliment you, and ask about your interests, and he's slow to jump in to talk or give you advice. He's not bashful, but he just enjoys listening more than he does being on stage. Almost everyone he knows describes him as "an excellent conversationalist." We can all learn from such fine people.

Obtaining Vital Information

If you love to listen, you will gain knowledge and if you incline your ear, you will become wise.

SIRACH

Besides building strong rapport, the other key reason to develop listening skills is to get the vital information needed to make a sale. Sales experts clearly recognize that knowledge is power. The more information you have concerning your sales situation, the greater your chances are of beating your competition and clinching the sale. Selling can be compared to putting together a puzzle where each piece of information received from a prospect is a piece of the puzzle. As the pieces are connected together, an entire picture evolves.

The goal of a salesperson is to absorb a tremendous amount of relevant information in the shortest possible period of time. This is necessary to qualify the prospect quickly (determine if he can and will eventually buy the product), come up with a solution to the prospect's problems, and present the solution in a better way than your competition did.

When a prospect first meets a salesperson, the prospect is reluctant to share information immediately. The prospect has not yet had the opportunity to develop trust or rapport with the salesperson. The prospect is like a faucet that gives only a trickle of information (see Illustration 6). When a salesperson uses strong, active listening, the prospect starts to loosen up and feel more comfortable with the salesperson. The prospect's defensiveness lessens and he no longer feels the salesperson is there for a sales pitch. As a result, the trickle of information from the prospect can often turn into a gusher, providing the salesperson with a wealth of vital information.

ILLUSTRATION 6
PROSPECT'S REACTION TO WEAK
AND STRONG LISTENING SKILLS

WEAK LISTENING:

STRONG LISTENING:

INFORMATION
BURSTS OUT —
FLOW IS STRONG
AND STEADY.

TRICKLE OF
INFORMATION.

PROSPECT IS TURNED *OFF*

- CLAMS UP — HOLDS BACK
- REMAINS COOL, GUARDED, DEFENSIVE
- DOES NOT VOLUNTEER INFORMATION
- MAY PROVIDE MISLEADING INFORMATION
- GIVES BASIC DATA — NOTHING OF SUBSTANCE
- SEES SALESPERSON AS INTRUDING, INTERRUPTING
- RUSHES SALESPERSON OUT

PROSPECT IS TURNED FULL *ON*

- FREELY VOLUNTEERS INFORMATION
- WANTS TO COOPERATE
- IS STRAIGHTFORWARD
- SHARES INSIDE INFORMATION, INTIMATE FEELINGS, OPINIONS, ATTITUDES
- ENJOYS BEING WITH SALESPERSON
- VIEWS SALESPERSON AS A VALUABLE RESOURCE
- MAKES RECOMMENDATIONS TO HELP SALESPERSON

The chapter on questioning and probing includes detailed insights on the types of information that will give you the important edge in selling. Here are just a few of the many areas that a salesperson needs to probe into and listen for to develop a foundation of information:

• The prospect's business needs, problems, and goals, and his priorities for each

• The prospect's personal motives and aspirations

• Qualifying (buying) criteria, such as money available to spend, time frame in which to make a buying decision, approval process required to authorize the purchase, and main competition for the sale

• Technical specifications required of your product

• Information about the prospect's company, such as financial history, products or services it provides, business philosophy, goals, problems, ideals, organizational structure, and key decision-makers

The more information that you possess about the prospect and his organization, the better able you are to create strategies to counter possible product objections, concerns, or questions and eliminate your competition; develop a strong proposal and presentation that demonstrates an excellent fit between the prospect's needs and wants and your product or service; and use your time effectively by spending it on selling opportunities that will yield the greatest amount of sales, both short-term and long-term.

Careful listening for subtle clues can alert a salesperson to large opportunities before his competition is aware of it. Often a prospect makes some offhand remark or drops some faint hint that is the vital key to a profitable sale. In general, the more a salesperson knows about his prospect's company and its competitors, the more valuable he is in the eyes of his prospect. Credibility is increased because the salesperson has made an investment of time and effort to learn about the account and to develop a business relationship with that organization. Knowing a company and working with its staff to solve their problems and help meet their goals with your product or service means that you become a valuable business advisor: a service-oriented account manager as opposed to a sell-'em-and-leave-'em salesperson.

Finally, there's another very important category of information to learn and absorb, and that is the information you continually learn about your own company and its products or services. In addition, most smart companies, even small ones, send their salespeople to training courses. Regardless of how long they have been selling, salespeople should constantly seek to enhance their sales knowledge and techniques. Whether by attending an in-house presentation or an outside training seminar, developing effective listening skills will help you to accumulate information that you can use later to make your career more successful.

> *From listening comes wisdom, and from speaking repentance.*
>
> ITALIAN PROVERB

Making Selling Easier

Listening can make the first meeting with a prospect progress smoothly. One of the advantages of spending more time listening is that it takes some of the pressure off a salesperson. Talking has historically been the trademark of the salesperson. Although salespeople enjoy speaking, it's often quite difficult to perform all the time. Typically, the most awkward time for salespeople is when they first meet a prospect. As happens when we meet anyone, there is an initial interpersonal relationship tension; you feel some degree of nervousness. You know the feeling. You're at a party and the hostess introduces you to Dave Jenkins. She suddenly says, "Oops, I forgot to get extra ice cubes. I'll be back later," and leaves you stranded with Dave. After a few minutes of awkwardness, the tension usually starts to melt away as you get to know each other and feel more comfortable.

When we first meet someone, we search for areas of commonality with that person. Listening and asking open-ended questions to get your prospect talking freely is an excellent way to begin a sales interview in a comfortable, friendly way. It makes the approach so much easier on the salesperson, and relaxes the prospect as well. When a salesperson asks relevant questions of the prospect and then sits back and listens, he doesn't have to worry immediately about what he has to say next, as he would if he were talking non-stop. Unfortunately, many salespeople believe that they have to talk constantly for the first ten minutes to get their pitch in. But consider the following approach.

After initially exchanging amenities with the prospect, the salesperson says, "Mr. Prospect, I studied your annual report before coming here, and I'm quite impressed. Your company's revenues have been growing at a tremendous pace—about 44 percent average annual growth over the last five years. What are your feelings on whether that growth rate will continue over the next five years?" A question like that can get the prospect talking for several minutes while providing a wealth of information to help in the sale. The prospect appreciates being asked his opinion on what appears to be an important question. The salesperson can then relax for a couple of minutes.

In addition to relieving the pressure of constantly talking, listening makes it easier for the salesperson to gather composure, think about his next question, analyze what's going on, and respond appropriately to the prospect.

Listening also enables a salesperson to get more information faster and more accurately, thus reducing the need to revisit the prospect or make needless telephone calls. Time management and qualifying is improved, which translates into being able to visit more prospects. Listening and using feedback questions reduces misunderstandings and false expectations, thus helping to avoid problems before they can develop. In addition, listening helps a salesperson read buying signals and close a sale faster.

Improving Your Image

> *When in the company of sensible people, we ought to be doubly cautious of talking too much, lest we lose two good things—their good opinion and our own improvement.*

> WALTER COLTON

A salesperson's primary personal goal is to make an excellent first impression with his prospect and then to maintain that professional image throughout the relationship. When a prospect likes, respects, and trusts a salesperson, a solid, beneficial relationship is built. A positive relationship can be an important deciding factor in choosing one salesperson's products or services over another's. Listening will probably do more to help your personal and professional image than just about any other interpersonal skill.

When we think of that rare person, the excellent listener, we probably associate certain major traits with that person. A good listener is typically thought of as a person who is caring, considerate, trustworthy, tactful, discreet, reasonable, open-minded, and sincere. It's astounding how the mere act of listening extremely well can create such a positive impression of a person. To illustrate further how powerful listening can improve the image of the listener, look at the following additional traits listed below. Ask yourself if you would describe an accomplished listener as a person probably having some or most of these traits:

- alert
- confident
- wise
- thoughtful
- mannerly
- patient
- forgiving
- friendly
- conscientious

- cooperative
- self-controlled
- relaxed
- perceptive
- rational
- intelligent
- dependable
- ethical
- humble

A salesperson who is a good listener shows that he is there to hear the prospect and to help, as opposed to the stereotypical image of the fast-talking, glib salesperson who is pushy and always trying to "sell" the prospect. For a moment, picture the talkative, high-pressure salesperson who is always trying to get a word in edgewise, not letting a prospect give his opinion or vent his feelings. The salesperson with poor listening skills might project certain undesirable traits to the prospect. Would you perhaps think of a salesperson who is a very poor listener as possessing some or many of these following traits?

- aggressive
- arrogant/boastful
- absent-minded
- aloof
- sneaky
- impatient
- critical

- opinionated
- outspoken
- intolerant
- hasty
- nervous
- quarrelsome
- brash

Being a poor listener certainly does not mean that a person actually possesses any of these traits. However, in many ways, poor listening creates a negative impression of a person, and a description of that person would probably include a few negative personal characteristics that could jeopardize or kill a sale.

Most salespeople are neither excellent nor extremely poor listeners, but somewhere in between. Developing strong listening skills will work wonders in improving the positive impression you make on your prospect, helping to establish your credibility, and reinforcing your overall professionalism.

Defusing Tense Situations

Listening is a powerful skill that can calm people quickly. Every salesperson occasionally has to deal with irate prospects. They may be upset (angry, disappointed, impatient) for a number of justified or unjustified reasons. Sometimes it's because the salesperson made a mistake; an incorrect product was ordered or an important delivery date that was agreed upon was missed. The salesperson might have forgotten to notify the prospect of an additional expense that is included with an order. Or it may be something as common as a salesperson forgetting to return a phone call that appears to be routine but is considered important by the prospect. On the other hand, it may be that the prospect blatantly misunderstood what the salesperson said or had unrealistic expectations about a product or service but won't admit it. A prospect's anger and emotional state might not even have anything to do with the salesperson: the prospect might have just had an unpleasant experience, such as a chewing-out from his boss or an argument with a cab driver. Whatever the reason, the second the prospect sees the salesperson or talks to him on the phone, *bang*—an explosion of emotional fireworks. The prospect begins shouting, pointing an accusing finger at the salesperson, or displaying other aggressive, intimidating body language gestures.

According to transactional analysis, an angry person is either in a parent state or a child state. In the parent state, the prospect acts as the authority figure or disciplinarian who scolds or punishes the "naughty" salesperson by giving him a lecture or threatening to cancel the present order and withhold future business from him. If the prospect is in the child state, he will have temper tantrums in which his attitude is selfish, unreasonable, demanding, and opinionated. Almost every statement he makes will contain the word *I*—"I want," "I know," "I demand." Your goal is to get the angry prospect to the adult state where you can carry on a rational, intelligent conversation that can enable both of you to look at the situation logically and resolve the problem in a mutually acceptable way.

On first meeting a seething customer, a salesperson can react in a number of ways. The first is to become angry or emotional in return, raising his voice, making counter-accusations, disagreeing, arguing, or returning threats. This response can be very tempting when a salesperson has irrefutable proof that the customer is wrong or when the salesperson couldn't care less about losing the business account. Illustration 7 shows what happens to the customer's emotional level if a salesperson becomes equally emotional or argumentative. Saying the following to the prospect can only fan the flames of unproductive emotions: "It's not my fault." "Calm down." "Take it easy." "I don't have to listen to this." "I think you're being unreasonable." "You're wrong." "You're blowing this way out of proportion." "You misunderstood me." "You apparently weren't listening when I said that."

When a salesperson argues with a customer, feelings are hurt; egos clash. Each feels the need to win at the expense of the other. The result is that the customer

ILLUSTRATION 7
SALESPERSON ARGUES

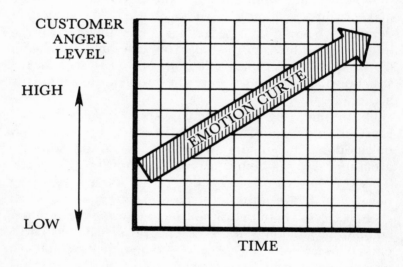

becomes angrier and more unreasonable and the sale is lost. What may have been a long-term relationship is damaged beyond repair. Arguing or displaying other negative emotions—defensiveness, annoyance, impatience—with a prospect is not only unprofessional, it doesn't do any good. The whole situation becomes a never-ending downward spiral leading to deterioration in communication.

The next type of behavior that many salespeople resort to knowingly or unknowingly when dealing with an angry customer is interrupting the customer and trying to offer some explanation, calm the prospect down, or propose an instant solution. In this situation, the salesperson is not reacting negatively to the prospect; rather, he wants to jump right into a blazing emotional inferno to fix the situation. Illustration 8 shows two possible emotional curves for the prospect. When a salesperson repeatedly interrupts a customer, not letting him finish a sentence or vent his emotions, the anger level remains constant. The prospect does not calm down. Though interrupting is certainly not as explosive as arguing, damage still results. Salespeople sometimes interrupt with statements like "Yeah, I know, but...," "Look, I'm trying to help, if you'd give me a chance," "Let me just say that...," or "I hear you, but let me explain that...."

The second emotion curve in Illustration 8 (fluctuating up and down) shows what happens when a salesperson alternates between listening to and interrupting the prospect before he has fully cooled down. The moment the salesperson begins actively listening, the prospect's anger level goes down. When the salesperson stops listening and interrupts, the anger level starts climbing. This frustrating cycle may be repeated many times. Both curves on the chart clearly illustrate that interrupting the prospect will not resolve a tense situation, but may prolong it at the expense of a business or personal relationship.

ILLUSTRATION 8
SALESPERSON INTERRUPTS

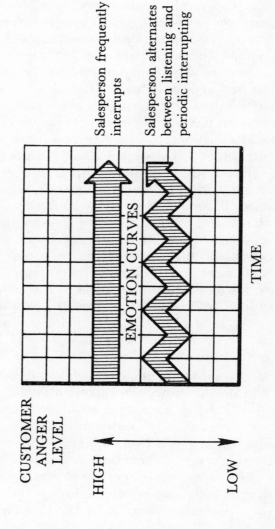

CUSTOMER
ANGER
LEVEL

HIGH

LOW

EMOTION CURVES

Salesperson frequently
interrupts

Salesperson alternates
between listening and
periodic interrupting

TIME

The third way a salesperson can react to an emotional or angry prospect is the best option: complete listening. It's not only quick, but it's also a very productive way to resolve a heated situation. You can't get into an argument or fight if one person is listening. Listening is the best way to defuse a ranting and raving or disappointed prospect, because it enables him to vent his anger—to get it completely off his chest. Emotional people possess an overwhelming need to have their say. Pride, ego, and personal integrity may feel threatened. Some wise salespeople actually encourage prospects to release their pent-up frustrations, because they realize that nothing can be accomplished until the unproductive emotional level is brought down quickly.

A prospect with a real or imagined grievance comes on pretty strong when he starts discussing it with you. Listening accomplishes the important goals of relaxing him, taking him off the defensive, slowing him down, and reducing friction. Illustration 9 shows the effect on the prospect's anger level when a salesperson listens intently and sincerely and does not interrupt or argue, but lets the prospect fully express his feelings before trying to address and resolve the issue. However, if the salesperson fakes listening, the prospect may become even angrier, feeling that he is being manipulated and made a fool of.

Listening is a soothing activity. The salesperson who listens shows the prospect that he's open-minded, non-judgmental, and interested in a peaceful resolution of the problem. Active listening immediately begins to alleviate the problem by giving the customer a chance to talk it through and thus experience emotional release. Listening tells the other person that his feelings are being carefully considered. If your prospect is wrong about something, listening to him or her does not mean that you are agreeing with him. It simply means that you're giving

ILLUSTRATION 9
SALESPERSON LISTENS

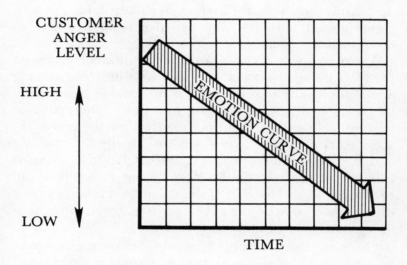

CUSTOMER
ANGER
LEVEL

HIGH

LOW

EMOTION CURVE

TIME

him a fair opportunity to state his side of the story before you address each of his concerns.

Nor does listening to an angry prospect imply that the salesperson is subservient to the prospect or that he is a whipping boy. No salesperson should ever stand by and listen if a prospect is dishing out personal abuse—attacking the principles, morals, or personality of the salesperson. Calling a salesperson incompetent or a moron or using swear words or vulgar terms to describe him is sufficient reason for the salesperson to explain in direct terms that he will not tolerate being called names or otherwise demeaned and that he is interested in helping the prospect, but will leave immediately if the abuse continues.

Handling the emotional customer by listening fully will reap many rewards. It helps the prospect save face. Therefore, the listener is greatly appreciated for his consideration. The salesperson's credibility increases because he remains in control, shows great composure under fire, doesn't judge or take lightly what the prospect says, and, above all, acts like a professional. Listening creates a sense of obligation on the part of the prospect to be reasonable—to work with the salesperson because he was cooperative enough to put up with the prospect's behavior. When a prospect goes on ranting and raving without interruption, he may feel uncomfortable with himself. He may feel guilty about taking his anger out unjustifiably on the salesperson, or he may see himself as foolish and unreasonable after listening to his tirade.

Persuading the Prospect

One of the best ways to persuade others is with your ears—by listening to them.

DEAN RUSK

Many salespeople are taught that persuasion is a one-way process in which a salesperson tells his side of the story and the prospect becomes convinced after the salesperson finishes. Most books written about giving speeches and presentations have a chapter on how to persuade your audience; therefore, it's natural to equate persuasion with one person attempting to influence another by his speech. Today, however, just being a smooth talker won't work with the sophisticated, knowledgeable buyers out there.

Since ancient Greek and Roman times, people were taught oratorical techniques whereby they were advised on how to create an argument in order to persuade their audience to agree with their side of an issue. Yet today, some salespeople still say to their prospects, "Let me explain my argument [not reasons] for installing our new paint-spraying equipment in your factory."

Certainly, designing and delivering a convincing sales presentation is almost always necessary to get a sale. However, good listening can also be very persuasive. Persuasion is a technique used to get your prospect to agree that your product can be a great vehicle to solve his problems or meet certain needs. However, no amount of persuasive sales talk will do a bit of good unless your prospect is in a receptive frame of mind—until he is willing to analyze objectively what you're proposing. There's a saying in selling: "A man convinced against his will is of the same opinion still." That's why it's critical to set the stage so that the prospect will at least be willing to consider your message.

When you actively and sincerely listen to your prospect, it shows that you are trying to be open-minded and reasonable about anything he has to say. The law of psychological reciprocity comes into play. What this means is, if you respect the prospect by listening completely and agreeing with him whenever possible, he, in turn, will accord you the same courtesy by listening to you in an unbiased, cooperative way, and he will feel impelled to agree with you more.

As mentioned previously, prospects who are being listened to greatly appreciate the salesperson and are more likely to respond favorably to the person who concentrates on them. We all like agreeable people and shy away from disagreeable people. And the receptive frame of mind generated by listening enables the salesperson to be more persuasive. A salesperson may have the most sensible, logical presentation to give, but if the prospect is unwilling to listen, his thoughtful proposal is useless. Also, when a salesperson listens carefully and establishes good rapport with a prospect, the prospect is less willing to bring up minor objections or look at the salesperson's proposal in a highly critical way. Prospects tend to forgive small weaknesses in a salesperson's proposal if they like and respect the salesperson.

Prospects can sometimes convince themselves of the merits of our product or service if we listen and let them talk themselves into it. I remember one sales call where I was dealing with a very talkative prospect who wouldn't let me get in a word edgewise. I don't think he paused even once. He apparently liked me very much, as I was practicing good listening with him (which was very difficult, because he rambled on and on). I did not get a chance to talk about the benefits of his using our computers in his organization, so in a desperate attempt I interrupted and asked him, "Mr. Prospect, how do you see our computers specifically helping your company?" Eureka, I hit the mother lode! As I listened very intently again, the prospect did two wonderful things: he gave me a wealth of information, and he actually began to talk himself into the benefits of installing my computers in his organization. The more he persuaded himself, the more I "rewarded" him by listening. I got the sale shortly thereafter.

Psychiatrists, psychologists, and counselors use listening to help people arrive at their own conclusions. Carl Rogers, a noted psychologist, said, "If I can listen to what he tells me, if I can understand how it seems to him, if I can sense the emotional flavor which it has for him, then I will be releasing potent forces of change within him."

Listening is also very persuasive toward the end of the sales process when a salesperson asks a closing question and waits for a response. Prospects often stall by saying something like, "It sounds OK, but I don't think we really need it right away," or "I think we'll look around a bit more at some other companies before we make a decision." When a prospect stalls and seems to be indecisive, good listening will strongly demonstrate to the prospect that the salesperson is not afraid to handle that doubt or slight resistance. A good listener shows that he is confident that his product is the best solution for the prospect's problems or needs. This rock-steady poise will rub off on the prospect and often help persuade the prospect to reconsider and buy.

During a stall, the salesperson should not immediately make a desperate attempt to regain the close by launching into an explanation of why the prospect should buy. The salesperson pushes, the prospect pushes back, and no progress is made. Instead, a salesperson should probe carefully into why the prospect seems to be hesitating and listen empathetically to the last-minute doubts of the prospect. By doing so, the salesperson subtly but strongly shows that he cares, he understands and, most important of all, that he is not worried about the prospect's doubts because he knows the prospect will make the decision to buy. Showing nervousness by talking quickly to try to overwhelm the prospect into buying can only increase the prospect's feeling that making a decision may not be a good idea after all.

The benefits you will receive from improved listening will increase your sales, advance your career, and vastly improve your relationships with people in business, in social situations, and at home. You'll see how working at good listening can truly enrich your life.

3

Obstacles to Effective
Listening

The benefits received from good listening are many, but developing and maintaining active listening skills is not easy. Listening is a physical, mental, and emotional experience, and as such, certain obstacles and barriers interfere with good listening. As salespeople, we should be aware of the impediments to listening and work toward minimizing them. In both the short and the long run, the effort will be rewarded by increased sales and improved personal and business relationships. We should be aware of obstacles to effective listening such as those that follow.

Feelings about the Speaker

If a listener has negative feelings about the person speaking, it's difficult to listen openly and objectively. Certain characteristics exhibited by the speaker may bother the listener to the extent that they overshadow what is being said. For example, the listener may look down upon the speaker's clothes, grooming, posture, or some other aspect of his or her physical appearance. Also, the way the speaker talks may interfere with the listener's concentration. The speaker may talk too quickly or slowly or have an unpleasant voice (monotonous, harsh, or squeaky) or a heavy accent. A listener may judge a speaker by his delivery style, thus negatively perceiving him as too nervous, boring, aggressive, sarcastic, or arrogant.

A listener may read a speaker's body language and decide that the speaker is sloppy, weak, intimidating, or unfriendly. Or there may be a potential personality clash between speaker and listener. This is one of the most difficult listening barriers to overcome. It's easy to dismiss a valid concept or important piece of information because we think of someone as a jerk, a weirdo, stupid, snobbish, stiff, or impersonal.

Finally, differences in culture, age, sex, education, background, and values can create obstacles to open and receptive listening. It's always easier to listen and relate to people with whom we have much in common and whom we like and respect.

Bias Toward the Subject

If a listener has strong feelings about a certain subject and the speaker has contrary views (with the same degree of conviction), it can bring listening to a quick halt. Politics is the perfect example of this. Picture a diehard capitalist talking with a dedicated, lifelong communist, each trying to convince the other of the values and benefits of his own political/economic system. From a sales perspective, a salesperson might be trying to convince his prospect to automate his operations with a certain type of machinery, but the prospect feels automation is not the way to go. The prospect's built-in bias could finish the conversation immediately.

In cases where listener and speaker have different views on a subject, it's usually because each has had different exposure to the topic—knowledge, experience, and education. Each person, because of the strength of his convictions, will believe that his ideas, feelings, and ways of doing things are totally correct. He will then usually dismiss the other person's views and feelings on the topic of discussion as naive, wrong, unrealistic, nearsighted, or idealistic. It's impossible for any of us to have a completely open mind on a topic, unless we have had no exposure to it at all.

In the case of the salesperson trying to convince his prospect to automate his operations, the salesperson sees the business benefits of improved productivity, lower production costs, and better manufacturing quality. The prospect, on the other hand, who may view his operation as functioning reasonably well, sees automation as costly, disruptive to his production line, a source of morale problems among workers, and difficult to install and use. Trying to listen actively and receptively to topics and ideas with which we disagree, for whatever reasons, is a terribly difficult thing to do, especially if powerful emotions are stirred.

Negative Messages or Criticism from Speaker

Anything that a speaker says that comes across as threatening, annoying, frustrating, disappointing, or frightening diminishes the listening efficiency of the listener. For example, an angry prospect disappointed by a salesperson may use a condescending, scolding tone of voice upon seeing him. Sarcasm from the prospect, an accusing tone of voice, or threats ("I'll never order from you again" or "If you don't straighten this mess out now, I'll get right on the phone to your manager") will cause listening levels to take a nosedive. It's natural for the listener to become personally defensive, offended, or angry in return, and these emotional states will block listening.

Another listening blockage concerns negative messages that affect the listener emotionally. Let's imagine that a prospect brings up a series of tough objections. It may be criticism about the salesperson's product, complaints about what poor service his company is rumored to have, or harsh statements about there not being the slightest need even to consider buying the product or service. Any of these can cause a listener to tune out. In general, we find it difficult to listen to anything that is painful or unpleasant, especially if it's true and we don't want to admit it.

Here are some examples of negative messages from a prospect:

—"I'm sorry, but we just had to cancel your order; budget cuts, you know."

—"Your price is way too high."

—"We were thinking about buying your product, but decided to go to a competitor."

—"I just don't like the way your product is made."

—"I know you have done a lot of work on your comprehensive sales proposal, but the vice president has decided to hold off on this project for a year or so."

When hearing something disappointing or feeling let down or "used," it's easy and natural for the listener to become overly sensitive and blow the situation out of proportion, overreacting in a way that can only make things worse.

Condition of Listener

A listener's physical, mental, and emotional condition can impede effective listening. Physical fatigue—whether caused by overwork, emotional stress, lack of sleep, or jet lag—can negatively affect a person's ability and desire to concentrate. Being sick or having some sort of physical ailment may aggravate an already bad situation. Eating a heavy lunch, especially with several alcoholic beverages, and then sinking into a plush, comfortable chair in a stuffy office may induce sleep rather than attention.

A listener cannot focus on a speaker's ideas if his mind is absorbed with his own thoughts, feelings, wishes, or problems. There could be something weighing on the listener's mind that annoys or upsets him. It could be the burden of ongoing marital or financial problems, family sickness, or emotional/psychological problems, or it could be some unpleasant recent experience that causes emotions to flare up such as getting a traffic ticket, finding out an expensive household appliance has broken down, or getting turned down for a promotion that he feels he deserved. When such personal conditions prevail, the attention and effort needed for effective listening are extremely difficult to muster.

Physical Environment

Your listening can be adversely affected by your surroundings and the events that are happening around you. Again, one of the keys to effective listening is to be able to concentrate fully on what the speaker is saying. Anything or anyone that affects that concentration or causes distractions is harmful.

One environmental condition that can hurt listening is room temperature and air circulation. If you're sitting in a room that is too hot, cold, stuffy, damp, or dry, especially for long periods, you will be uncomfortable. The natural tendency is to think about how bad you're feeling instead of what someone is talking about.

Another consideration is lighting. If the lighting in a room is bad—that is, if the sun is glaring through the windows right into your eyes or the lighting is subdued to the extent that it seems unnatural or uncomfortable— your listening will be affected.

Next is the problem of noise and acoustics. If distracting noise is competing with the speaker, it can tax a listener's energy, and if the noise continues for long periods of time, it's likely to make the listener tune out what's being said. Distracting sounds include noise from outside the building, traffic in the hallway, a noisy air conditioner or circulating fan, background music, office machinery, and constant telephone ringing. Poor acoustics in a room can cause excessive echoes or absorb sounds, which makes voices sound dull or muffled. Poor room acoustics increase the energy it takes to listen.

Office decor can also affect listening effectiveness. If a prospect's office is sloppy, cluttered, or poorly decorated, it can distract the listener and also reflect negatively on the competence or importance of the prospect. At the other extreme, if an office is extremely attractive, with artwork, fine furniture, plush carpeting, and exotic plants, it will tempt a listener to glance around and become sidetracked by the rich surroundings. A prospect's office may be on the upper floor of a skyscraper with a large picture window overlooking the city, or it may be an office in a rural setting with a window overlooking a beautiful outdoor country scene. The temptation to look, not listen, is hard to resist.

Indifference or Boredom

A talkative prospect whose conversation drifts in various directions may seem boring to the salesperson who is actively trying to listen but is having a hard time finding relevant information among all the extraneous details. When a prospect goes off on a tangent and takes a long time to make a point, it's difficult for the salesperson to maintain a high listening level.

Even if a speaker is a good communicator, the content of his talk may be boring to the listener. As a consequence, the listener may dismiss the information as being un-important to the sales interview. Sometimes a prospect talks in detail about his company's organization and history or about technical subjects that are too complicated for an uninformed salesperson to comprehend. The result is an indifferent salesperson who is not actively listening, even though there may be important facts or ideas buried within the prospect's monologue. When a listener is bored, indifferent, or aloof, his attention span shortens and the subject of the speaker's talk escapes him.

Overall, there are many obstacles that must be overcome to make good listening happen. Poor listeners fall prey to them easily; good listeners recognize them and compensate for them by trying doubly hard to concentrate on the proper listening skills highlighted in the following chapter.

4

14 Effective Listening Techniques

Were we as eloquent as angels,
yet we should please more men and women
much more by listening than by talking.

WALTER COLTON

Most of us take listening for granted, even though we do it every day throughout our lives. Poor listening is usually unintentional and simply stems from bad habits. One of the gravest errors that some people can make is to assume that they have no listening problems. Since there are so many elements necessary for effective listening, practically everybody has some type of major listening weakness. Also, many people unfortunately feel that the responsibility for successful communication rests with the person doing the talking. Because they feel that the speaker has a vested interest in what he or she is saying, they think that the listener can be totally passive. But the listener actually has a larger responsibility in the communication process; if he doesn't understand something, it's up to him to ask the speaker for an explanation.

Becoming an effective listener takes time and effort. It's never too late to learn to listen, and you'll find its rewards extremely worthwhile. You've already taken the first positive step by reading this book. This chapter contains 14 valuable ways to improve your listening capabilities. Don't try to improve in all of these areas at once; take just two or three listening techniques and practice them as much as you can for the next two to four weeks. Once you feel confident that you've mastered them, practice two or three more for the next several weeks while continuing to use and reinforce the previous techniques you've developed. Keep on slowly but steadily building up this pyramid of listening skills.

Like any skill, you'll find that these listening techniques come naturally after a while. Even after a few short weeks of enhancing your listening, you'll see a difference in dealing with your prospects and an improvement in your personal relationships. The full impact, though, may take months of determined effort. Consider asking your spouse, friends, or co-workers to help you improve your listening abilities. After all, they're probably the best judges of your listening skills.

Listening is a complicated activity that typically involves four general steps: 1. physically hearing the speaker's words and tone of voice; 2. concentrating on understanding what the speaker is meaning to say; 3. analyzing, verifying, and weighing the information received; and 4. determining how to appropriately respond to it.

There are 14 ways (which fall within those four general steps) that I recommend to improve overall listening skills.

1. Make a commitment to listen.
2. Do not interrupt or finish someone's sentence.
3. Use reflective phrases and statements.
4. Don't fake listening.
5. Resist distractions.
6. Use feedback/paraphrasing and summarizing.
7. Take selective notes.
8. Use favorable body language when listening.

9. Judge the content of the message, not the person delivering it.
10. Analyze and evaluate; listen for main ideas and determine the overall meaning.
11. When the situation gets hot, keep cool and listen.
12. Use empathetic listening.
13. Listen for vague or incomplete information and for important sales cues.
14. Listen for and observe buying signals.

The rest of the chapter tells you specifically how to improve in each of these techniques.

LISTENING TECHNIQUE 1:
Make a Commitment to Listen

The ears don't work until the tongue has expired.

ANONYMOUS

Listening is hard work that takes determination and energy. In addition to being mentally and psychologically challenging, careful listening affects the body physically. It produces an increased heart rate, faster blood circulation, and a rise in body temperature.

The first step in improving your listening is to make a firm commitment to work at making your listening more effective. You can improve your listening skills by concentrating on them one at a time, every day, every time you listen. You'll notice positive reactions from your friends and prospects immediately and you'll eventually benefit in your relationships with them.

Here are some suggestions for increasing your ability to listen effectively:

● Work to improve your listening during *all* social occasions, not only when dealing with prospects. Use the listening skills explained in this chapter when listening to your spouse, friends, relatives, and co-workers.

• Prepare yourself mentally to listen. Remind yourself each time you listen to concentrate on your purpose and clear your mind of all distracting thoughts.

• Prepare yourself physically to listen. Assume a comfortable standing or sitting position, but don't slouch while standing or slump in the chair.

• Prepare yourself emotionally to listen. Remind yourself that you are to judge the information, not the speaker. Also, think positively and treat the speaker's information or opinion as unique, interesting, and valuable.

It's a good idea to motivate yourself constantly to listen. One of the reasons why some people are very good listeners and others are mediocre is purpose. Effective listeners see a positive purpose to their listening. They see themselves gaining information or understanding feelings that will somehow benefit them—if not immediately, then in the future. Telling yourself that there is a valid, even selfish reason to listen can help stimulate your attention span.

LISTENING TECHNIQUE 2:
Do Not Interrupt or Finish Someone's Sentence

One of the quickest and surest ways for a salesperson to cut off the flow of precious information from a prospect is to interrupt a prospect repeatedly.This demonstrates a clear lack of courtesy for the person speaking, breaks the speaker's train of thought, is frustrating for the speaker, and gives a negative impression of the salesperson.

When a prospect describes a problem, need, or goal that your product or service is perfectly suited for, the temptation to jump in and say "Wait a minute, we have *exactly* what you need" may be irresistible. It's a human tendency to want to interrupt a conversation when we are excited or quickly reminded of a point triggered by what the prospect is saying, but it's a bad idea to do so.

Interrupting a prospect during a calm discussion is bad enough, but if a salesperson interrupts when the customer is angry or disappointed and needs to vent his feelings, this is tantamount to throwing gasoline on a fire. Or when a person shares personal feelings or exclusive information that he considers very important, interrupting him will cause him to stop sharing his viewpoint—to give up out of sheer frustration with the so-called listener.

There are two types of interruptions. One is the blatant, rude kind in which a listener breaks into people's conversations. The second kind of interruption is less abrupt, but nevertheless it is an annoying, inconsiderate gesture. It occurs when a listener lets a speaker finish his sentence, but does not respond in any meaningful way to what the speaker has said. Instead, the listener begins a new conversation or makes a quick remark unrelated to what the speaker has just said. In either case, the speaker feels that his remarks were either totally ignored or not important enough to comment on further.

Besides interrupting, another bad habit to avoid is finishing a person's sentence. Salespeople usually do this with slow-talking prospects who repeatedly pause and seem to take forever to make a point. It's terribly frustrating for a salesperson to listen to this type of prospect, especially if the salesperson is rushed for time and needs to get a lot of information from the prospect. There are two problems that result from frequently completing a person's sentence: first, you may be dead wrong about what the person is intending to say, and second, if you do it often enough, your prospect will become annoyed at your affront to his intelligence.

Another problem is the prospect who rambles on and on and never seems to say much. There are times when you have to interrupt the prospect because he is going off on a tangent or is becoming too detailed when it's not necessary. Perhaps the prospect is getting into an area that is leading away from the sale—talking in glowing terms about your competition, or making negative comments about your company or its products. Under these non-productive conditions, you have to refocus the prospect and either direct him to areas you want to talk about or bring the rambling to a close.

Quite a few suggestions in this book will improve listening, but if you are one of those who interrupts or tries to speak for others, improvement in just this one area will quickly result in positive responses from the people you deal with. Interrupting is a habit that many listeners are not aware of when they're doing it, and like any habit, it can be broken with perseverance. Here are some suggestions.

• To avoid interrupting a person in midsentence, actively concentrate on allowing that person to finish his thought completely. A simple technique is to wait 2-4 seconds after a speaker ends a statement and then respond. According to Dr. Gerald Goodman, a psychology professor at UCLA, slowing the conversation down a bit relaxes the person you're talking with. Professor Goodman calls the time between the end of one person's statement and the beginning of the other person's statement the "inter-response boundary." Dr. Goodman says that this little interval of time, which may seem like a long wait for some listeners, gives the speaker a sense of not being pressured; it also shows that the listener has respect for the speaker's opinions.

• Ask a friend or your spouse to point out every time you interrupt him or her. Your willingness to improve annoying habits will be appreciated.

• Instead of abruptly changing the subject, acknowledge

and respond to what the speaker has just said. Bring the present topic to a natural close before approaching new areas of interest.

• When emotions on both sides are running high and you feel that the prospect is wrong, suppress the urge to "correct" his misguided impressions.

• If a speaker pauses briefly, don't rush in to fill the silence. Wait for him to finish organizing his thoughts and expressing them, until you are sure that he has completely finished his sentence.

• Avoid filling in someone's sentences. Grin and bear it; you can't change someone's speech pattern or personality.

To refocus a rambling prospect, try this method. First, gently break into the prospect's conversation as soon as he finishes his sentence. ("Mr. Prospect...") Next, refer to a point the prospect made previously or make a leading statement that you would like him to talk about. You may also compliment the prospect at this step to get his attention and reduce his possible annoyance at your interruption. ("You said something rather interesting a while back that got me thinking. You said...") Finally, ask the prospect to respond to the previous reference. ("Could you talk about that a bit more?") This will redirect the prospect to talk about what you want him to. This step proves that you didn't interrupt for your own sake; after all, you gave the floor right back to your prospect.

Another technique to use with a rambling prospect is to again gently break into the conversation when the prospect finishes his sentence and quickly summarize what you think the main points are. After that, you can begin new areas of discussion. Here's an example.

> "Mr. Prospect, I can appreciate what you're saying. What it really seems to boil down to is that you've got several problems in that area and there's really nothing anyone

can do about it right now. I think, however, our products
can definitely help you in other areas and I'd like to get
your opinion on that. Let's discuss that for a while. In the
area of..."

Finally, another technique to use with a prospect who
launches into a seemingly never-ending monologue is to
ask him not to delve into too much unneeded detail
because of time limitations or priorities that you need to
cover. Here is an example of a salesperson refocusing his
prospect in this fashion.

"Ms. Prospect, if it's OK with you, what I'd like to do is get
a good overall picture of your business needs and problems
before we get into any amount of detail in one area. Could
we perhaps discuss what general manufacturing processes
you use and what types of problems you've been experiencing
and then later look into the specifics of each one?"

LISTENING TECHNIQUE 3:
Use Reflective Phrases and Statements

Have you ever talked to a prospect who was such an
intent listener that he never responded to you—just stared
at you with steely eyes and a blank or intimidating facial
expression? At first, you probably weren't sure if he
agreed or disagreed with you, and you became increasingly
uncomfortable as the sales call went on. This type of
prospect is often called a clam because he tightly shuts
himself up. He appears to be listening, yet does not react
to what the salesperson says. The salesperson feels it is
unfortunately necessary to pry the clam (prospect) out of
his shell.

The reverse is also true; some salespeople listen without
ever responding, which makes the prospect feel that he is
not getting through to the salesperson. The prospect may
feel he is being scrutinized or judged by the salesperson,
a destructive impression that inhibits rapport and reduces
the effectiveness of the conversation.

In order to avoid such pitfalls, listen actively by using reflective phrases such as "yes," "you're right," "I see your point," or "sure." These are key words that you occasionally interject while listening to indicate that you are attentive and that the prospect has your approval (if appropriate). More detailed reflective responses include such statements as "That's important to you, isn't it," "I can imagine how you felt," and "I'd like to hear more about that."

There are also negative impacting phrases that can upset a prospect. The result will be damaged rapport and a shutoff of the flow of information. Avoid these and other abrupt, inconsiderate statements: "Well, the problem with that idea is...," "Yeah, sure, I hear what you're saying, but...," or "I know you think that's important, but let's not worry about it now."

Combining reflective statements with nods, smiles, and empathetic facial expressions at the appropriate moments can have a strong positive effect on rapport and greatly encourage a prospect to speak about topics you want him to address. Conversely, withholding reflective statements when prospects approach areas that can hurt the progress of a sales call helps to minimize dialogue that may be harmful to the sale. As such, these statements can be used or withheld to steer a prospect toward or away from a certain path of conversation.

Frank Everett, a friend of mine who sold minicomputers for a large data processing company, used this listening skill to get prospects to continue to compliment his computers and company. If his prospect said, "A lot of people seem to think smaller machines are the way to go," he swiftly responded, "I agree with you completely; that trend is skyrocketing." He displayed sincere enthusiasm in tone of voice and physical gestures and emphasized the words *I agree*. He then let the prospect continue to speak. As the prospect talked further, saying, "We feel that it's a wise approach for us to investigate installing minicomputers in place of our large computers," Frank said, "It definitely is a wise decision! Progressive companies are doing just that." He also nodded and smiled, and his whole face brightened when the prospect made favorable comments that brought the sale closer. The prospect's face brightened as well from the positive response he received. If the prospect commented favorably about Frank's competition, Frank remained motionless and speechless—not nodding, leaning forward, or supporting the prospect's viewpoint with "uh huh" or "I see." He actively withheld approval and tried to discourage continuation of a line of thought that profited a competitor.

LISTENING TECHNIQUE 4:
Don't Fake Listening

Many prospects consider pretending to listen the rudest listening habit of all. This is odd when you consider that people usually pretend to listen because they don't want to be rude or offend the person speaking. By using a polite facade, they hope to give the impression that they are eagerly soaking up every word being spoken. But when salespeople fake listening, prospects often realize it quickly; they feel used and angry that their time has been wasted by an uninterested person.

Faking listening is bad for two reasons. First, you can miss some important information that may help clinch the sale. Second, if the prospect picks up on the charade, rapport will be damaged and the salesperson's credibility will be lost.

It's usually easy to tell when someone is faking listening. The signals include eyes darting around or fixed in a blank stare, nodding or saying "uh huh" at inappropriate moments, and not being able to answer a simple question about the topic being discussed. In extreme cases, you may have to call the person's name two or three times to get him back into the conversation.

All of us occasionally daydream and become distracted. Maybe we are tired or have other pressing problems burdening us; maybe the speaker is saying something we've heard many times before. If you are caught being inattentive, a graceful way of getting out of this embarrassing situation and repairing the damage to your credibility is to say something like this: "Ms. Prospect, I apologize. I was thinking about something you said earlier that caught my attention [be ready to mention what that was if the prospect asks] and I lost track of your last train of thought. Could you please go over that again?" At least you're explaining that you were preoccupied with the prospect's situation rather than an upcoming golf game, your next appointment, or whatever else is on your mind. Even if you aren't caught daydreaming, it's a good idea to make such a statement if you realize that you've missed something that you need to know. Of course, you're always better off to limit distractions and make a dedicated effort to avoid faking listening.

LISTENING TECHNIQUE 5:
Resist Distractions

I've already mentioned distractions as obstacles to effective listening. Many listeners can be temporarily diverted from their listening course not only by what they hear, but also by what they see. Poor listeners yield to distractions easily, even in sensitive prospect situations where they should be giving their undivided attention to the prospect. It's very annoying for the speaker to feel that what he is saying is less important than some minor distraction that crops up. This feeling of neglect is compounded when the listener constantly concentrates on everything around him instead of the speaker.

A good listener is always on guard to resist such common distractions as passersby, outside activity as seen through a window, telephones ringing, and appealing aspects of decor in the prospect's office. Some distractions are very tempting, especially if you view your prospect as verbose or boring. Instead of allowing distractions to sidetrack your listening, strengthen your resolve to listen and concentrate even harder.

One way to minimize distractions is to arrange for an environment that is conducive to listening. If you are calling on a prospect in his office and there's outside street noise, loud office machines clanking away, or people walking in and out, it's difficult to control these factors. There are, however, several ways to counteract a potentially negative situation. If you've been dealing with your prospect for a while and have established a comfortable business relationship, you might tactfully ask the prospect to:

—Close his door or close the window facing the street. You can preface your request by saying, "Joe, I want to make sure that I give you my undivided attention. Would it be OK with you if we closed the office door to provide us with a bit more privacy and quiet?"

—Have his secretary or operator hold most phone calls. Do not make this request the first time you meet a new prospect. Once you've developed a rapport with him, explain that your meeting is very important and that you want to listen carefully to what's being discussed. The prospect should not mind complying with your wishes. Try this approach: "Mary, we have 45 minutes to go over your requirements on factory automation prior to our company presenting our solution. It's very important for us to review this completely today because you will be out of town for two weeks. Would it be OK if we asked your secretary to hold all but your most critical calls during this time?"

—Schedule your meeting in a conference room away from distractions. Try to have the prospect reserve a conference room before you arrive to ensure that it will be available. If necessary, you can justify this by explaining that you're bringing some product brochures, bulky demonstration products, or other materials and both of you will need extra elbow room to work comfortably.

—Meet before or after regular working hours if the distractions are caused primarily by normal interruptions from coworkers and phone calls. Salespeople occasionally ask to meet with prospects as early as 7:30 A.M. or after 5 P.M.

You may have to invite your prospect to your office where you can eliminate distractions. Or invite him to a productive working lunch, to be held in a secluded area of a quiet restaurant where both of you can talk easily and you can listen intently.

LISTENING TECHNIQUE 6:
Use Feedback/Paraphrasing and Summarizing

Two major goals of good listening are to demonstrate to your prospect that you are attentive and to prove that you understand exactly what he has said. Feedback/paraphrasing and summarizing are the skills necessary to accomplish these objectives. By doing so, you also fill in any information gaps and allow the prospect to alter, clarify, and reinforce what he has previously said.

Effective listening techniques must consist of a bit more than a simple reassurance that you are paying attention. Feedback or paraphrasing leads to accuracy and clarity of communication between salesperson and prospect because it indicates a strong desire on the part of the salesperson to find out whether he has fully understood the prospect.

One problem causing misunderstanding is that we attach different shades of meaning to terms and ideas. For example, a prospect may say that he wants "more flexible" terms and conditions in the sales contract or that he is looking to deal with an "established, larger-sized company." The prospect knows exactly what he means by these desires, but the salesperson will think of his own interpretation of these requests, and the two often do not match. That's why it's very important for the salesperson and prospect to be in sync—to understand clearly and completely what the other means.

In feedback/paraphrasing, you restate what the prospect has said to you, but in your own words, so that both of you will have a common base of reference. Merely repeating a message in the prospect's words does not always reveal full understanding.

You should ask feedback questions ("Are you saying that...?") and make clarifying statements ("It seems that what you need is...") every couple of minutes or after each main point has been discussed. Don't naturally assume you understand; verify it. Here are some other examples of feedback questions for you to use:

- "Ms. Prospect, let me make sure that I fully understand what you've just stated to me. You said.... Is that it?"
- "Then you believe [feel, think, etc.] that..."
- "If I read you correctly, you're proposing that.... Is that the case?"
- "Am I on the right track in thinking that...?"

Another excellent way to clarify understanding and impress the prospect is to use strategic summaries. If a salesperson does his job effectively, the prospect will open up and provide a lot of information, especially at the beginning of the sales cycle. This is information that will then be processed and evaluated prior to the sales presentation. During strategic points in a sales call—such as after asking qualifying questions of the prospect, after getting technical specifications needed by the prospect, or at the conclusion of the call—a salesperson should give a brief but comprehensive summary. The reason is essentially the same as for prompting feedback: it shows that you've been listening and have a good grasp of what the prospect needs and wants. In addition, it refreshes the prospect's memory on any decisions made or commitments agreed upon.

A strategic summary should take the salesperson less than a minute to make and should be done approximately every 10-15 minutes during the sales call. In this way, both the salesperson and the prospect ensure that neither is going off on tangents or misunderstanding the other. Here is an example of a brief but important summary performed by a fleet truck salesperson after qualifying a prospect:

> "Mr. Prospect, as I understand it, you need 15 panel trucks for your business that can each carry 3,000-pound loads. You want fuel economy in the 10-15 miles per gallon range, and you want a vehicle that requires fewer than 10 hours of overall maintenance per month. You have $210,000 budgeted for the trucks, and you are responsible for making the decision to select what brand trucks you'll be using. You'll be selecting a vendor based on the reliability history of the trucks, the best price, and whether delivery is possible within 2 months. Have I stated all this correctly? Is there anything that I left out that is important to you or that I should be aware of?"

Here's another example of a brief and effective summary that a robotics salesperson might use after getting technical requirements from his prospect:

> "Mr. Prospect, I want to make absolutely sure that I have all the necessary information about your needs prior to submitting a preliminary proposal. You said that you needed

an assembly robot that has the following characteristics and features: 6-axis movement; electric actuator motors, not hydraulic; uptime reliability of at least 96 percent; placement accuracy to one-thousandth of an inch; and the ability to lift 45 pounds and move that weight to any programmed position within 2 seconds. Does that cover all of your technical requirements, or are there any others that I need prior to writing my proposal?"

If the summary is done correctly several times in a sales call, the prospect will surely be impressed. These summaries are green lights indicating go—you've passed this junction in the sales call. The summary implies that you understand what the prospect has said and are ready to move on to the next important area of discussion.

LISTENING TECHNIQUE 7:
Take Selective Notes

Proper note-taking can make a sales call more effective; recording ideas and information from a prospect can make selling faster and easier. Jotting down key information immediately means you won't have to go over the same information again at a later date because you forgot it or misunderstood it. In addition, note-taking is highly complimentary to the prospect, because it shows that the salesperson is paying attention to the discussion and believes that the prospect's position and personal opinions are important. However, if note-taking is done improperly, it can negatively affect rapport and hurt a sale.

Note-taking for salespeople usually falls into one of two extremes: it's either overdone or not done at all. Let's take a look at the first category—the salesperson who plays court stenographer, trying to write down everything the prospect says. His intentions are good; he wants to show the prospect that he cares about what's being discussed and doesn't trust his memory to recall accurately.

However, problems occur when a salesperson tries to take constant and voluminous notes. The prospect may feel uncomfortable at having each of his words recorded as if he were on trial. A salesperson's frantic scribbling does not create a relaxing environment for the prospect to share both business information and important personal feelings. Rapport with the prospect is hurt; how can you effectively carry on a relaxed and open conversation when you're busily writing at 180 miles an hour? The biggest drawback to excessive note-taking is lack of eye contact, a critical element in establishing and maintaining rapport. In addition, if you're not looking at the prospect, you can't read his body language, which can dramatically affect the tone and meaning of what is being said. Another reason is that it's almost impossible to give your full attention to what is now being said if you're always in a catch-up mode, trying to write down what was said ten seconds ago. You must concentrate totally on important points of the call in order to analyze and respond to them efficiently.

At the other end of the spectrum is the salesperson who visits the prospect and takes no notes whatsoever. He runs the risk of forgetting major and minor points that affect the sale or suggesting to the prospect that the salesperson doesn't feel the prospect's information is important enough to record on paper. Prospects often feel that they're wasting their time talking to someone who will probably ask the same questions at a later date because he didn't remember the answers the first time. The result is damaged credibility for the salesperson.

The best course of action is to take selective, judicious notes. Remember, the two goals in note-taking are to show the prospect that you care enough to make the effort to take notes and to assure that you walk away from a meeting with correct information to help you achieve your next meeting's goals and eventually close the sale.

Here are some suggestions on effective note-taking.

—Before taking notes, ask the prospect's permission to do so. Here's an example: "Ms. Prospect, would it be okay if I jotted down some notes occasionally? I want to make sure I understand and remember the important points that you bring up during our meeting."

—Take notes at appropriate times throughout the sales call. Note-taking is especially important during the first sales call to record qualifying information and other information necessary to design a strong sales presentation.

—Write down key words, phrases, and numbers designed to jog your memory. Stay away from complete and long sentences; they take too much time. Instead, highlight the important information mentioned by the prospect. After the call, you can use your outline-style notes to fill in the blanks and fill out the information while it's fresh in your memory.

—Take notes on important points like the names of high-level contacts, a company's organization chart, telephone numbers, major problems, and needs that the prospect has that your product can address. Also, take notes on requests from the prospect and commitments you make that must be followed up.

—During personal, sensitive, or critical parts of a sales call, stop writing for the moment and give the prospect your undivided attention. Show concern, understanding, and empathy by listening intently, maintaining good eye contact, leaning forward to show interest, and nodding.

—Refer to your notes at appropriate times during the call to help you summarize and clarify important points made by the prospect. Use your notes after the call to help prepare for the next call.

LISTENING TECHNIQUE 8:
Use Favorable Body Language
When Listening

Excellent listeners make use of body language (non-verbal communication) to reinforce their other listening skills. Your goals in using the right body language are to create a relaxed, trusting environment and to build rapport with the prospect. This encourages the prospect to continue to share information with you. In addition to verbal cues, your whole body should show that you are listening.

Chapter 5 gives details on how to use and interpret non-verbal communication. Here are a few suggestions and guidelines to help you enhance your listening skills through body language.

Eyes: Maintain strong eye contact with the prospect without staring. It should be friendly, natural eye contact as you would use in conversation with a friend. Avoid the shifty-eyed look with your eyes focused on the prospect but your head facing away. Also avoid staring out the window, into the hall, at your notes, or at an area of interest in the prospect's office. Maintaining eye contact is extremely important for developing rapport with the prospect because it shows interest and consideration. Failure to do so can damage trust, cause suspicion, and damage communication.

Facial expressions: Listen and try to have your facial expressions echo the mood and sentiments of the prospect. For example, smile when the prospect is happy, and look concerned when the prospect is distraught. Make frequent and appropriate use of nodding to show your acceptance of what the prospect is saying; this simple action prompts the prospect to carry on a productive conversation. Avoid frowns, scowls, and other judgmental looks. Be careful not to stick your chin out while raising your head (it makes you look pompous and arrogant) or tuck your chin into your neck and point your eyes upward in a holier-than-thou attitude.

Posture and body position: Sit upright in your chair, close to the prospect's desk. You should maintain a relaxed yet erect sitting position, not slouch or sit stiffly as if a piece of wood were glued to your back. Also, don't cross your arms across your chest in a defensive posture. This position makes you look intimidating, and you will appear to shut out the prospect's comments or concerns. Successful sales veterans sit as described above, with one leg crossed over the other and the hands either resting loosely over the chair's armrests or occupied by taking notes. Don't begin your sales call by sitting on the edge of your seat and leaning forward with your elbows resting on the prospect's desk. Many prospects feel uncomfortable or intimidated if a salesperson they've just met gets too close to them. Besides, sitting on the edge of your seat is not a comfortable position for listening. Sometimes, however, it is very effective to lean your body toward the prospect if the prospect is very concerned about something and is sharing personal feelings or sensitive information. Leaning forward is a supportive gesture that shows the salesperson's strong desire to listen; he seems to be straining to hear every word the prospect says.

Distracting mannerisms: As you listen, avoid gestures and mannerisms such as playing with a pencil or some object on the prospect's desk, twisting a ring, biting or picking fingernails, or tapping your foot on the floor. Avoid yawning. Another important point: *never* make a blatant attempt to stare at your watch. Many prospects are annoyed at this nonverbal insinuation that the salesperson's time is more valuable than the prospect's. Looking at one's watch (especially several times in quick succession) can easily break a prospect's concentration and hurt rapport, and it may bring the discussion to a premature halt. If you must gauge how much time is left to cover the remaining important issues or to make sure that you don't miss your next appointment, put the arm where your watch is on your note pad or knee and subtly glance down in that direction. It's more tactful to do this than to raise your watch to your face.

LISTENING TECHNIQUE 9:
Judge the Content of the Message, Not the Person Delivering It

Although empathetic listening, in which you identify with your prospect and utilize emotions to establish or improve rapport, is important, the majority of your listening should be controlled and impartial. All too often we form hasty first impressions of people. Imposing our emotions, prejudices, and attitudes upon another person can impede the listening process to the extent that we lose something along the way—maybe the value of the information or ideas being expressed—because we are distracted or somehow bothered by the person we're listening to.

If your prospect doesn't make a sterling first impression on you, hold your fire and hear him out. It's easy to become emotionally turned off or overstimulated, and these extremes cause ineffective listening. Strive not to criticize, judge, or underestimate the prospect because of his appearance, tastes, mannerisms, personality, or behavior. Initially, you may be bothered or even repulsed by people who:

—Dress sloppily, strangely, or distastefully in your opinion, or show a disregard for good grooming and hygiene. Albert Einstein had long, disheveled hair and was not exactly a stylish dresser, but he had one of the greatest minds of all time. If his colleagues or the public had avoided listening to him because of his grooming and appearance, it would have been a tragic scientific loss for mankind. All too often we may catch ourselves passing judgment on a person's appearance. ("Look at that frumpy outfit she has on. She'd look ten years younger if she just was more stylish." "Boy, is he sloppy. Looking at his shirt and tie, I can tell that he had spaghetti for lunch.")

—Has a physical appearance that we judge to be unattractive, extremely attractive, or amusing, causing us to think about the person's physical characteristics, not what is being said. ("I cannot believe the size of that guy's stomach. It's hanging all over his desk. How gross." "She is really good-looking. I wonder if she's single? Maybe I'll ask her to lunch."

—Demonstrates personality traits, behavior, or mannerisms we view as eccentric, unpleasant, or obnoxious. The speaker's personality may be the opposite of yours, which makes it hard for you to understand and empathize with him. A quiet, tactful, and gracious salesperson may find it tough to conquer the emotional listening barrier of dealing with an opinionated, crude, and domineering prospect. Or an amiable, caring, people-oriented prospect might be viewed as weak or undisciplined by a no-nonsense, formal, by-the-book type of salesperson.

—Has a speech delivery style that makes communication difficult. The disorganized speech habits of a prospect may overshadow the importance of the message. Poor speaking traits such as talking too fast without pausing or speaking at a snail's pace can frustrate or bore a listener. The tone of a speaker's voice may be shrill, grating, gravelly, or dreadfully monotonous. Mumbling, a heavy accent, mispronouncing words, vulgar language, or pompous-sounding words that blur meanings can also interfere with our listening. Try not to concentrate on how a person speaks. Just listen to the information being presented, regardless of how bad the presentation may be. There may be a golden selling clue buried underneath the mountain of poorly chosen statements. On the other hand, don't be easily swayed and charmed by someone who speaks well and makes an impressive appearance. Analyze the message of a smooth communicator; do not assume that because the delivery is effective, the content must be valid and useful. Just as poor speech habits do not necessarily mean a useless message, a glib tongue may not have any valid content behind it.

LISTENING TECHNIQUE 10:
Analyze and Evaluate; Listen for Main Ideas and Determine the Overall Meaning

He understands badly who listens badly.

WELSH PROVERB

As I've said previously, listening can often be compared to putting together a jigsaw puzzle. You have to take the hundreds (or thousands) of individual pieces and fit them together properly to make the final image. Listening is the same in the sense that you have to listen to details and facts and then piece them together to arrive at the prospect's overall message and intended meaning. Unlike a jigsaw puzzle, however, in listening you don't know the end result ahead of time. That's why it's important to listen carefully in order to make sure you get all the pieces and analyze and fit them together to make sense of the conversation.

It's a good idea to set listening objectives that give direction and focus to your listening efforts. Organized listening helps you get away from random, unstructured patterns of listening and reach your goals more quickly and completely. I've already discussed what to do when a prospect rambles on in a disorganized way. If this happens, it's still your job to piece the conversation together and determine what he is getting at. Studies show that only 25 percent of the people listening to any formal talk actually understand the speaker's central idea. Nobody wants to listen to sterile facts that by themselves have little or no meaning. It's important to listen for connecting ideas and overall key messages given by the prospect. Try to get the gist of what he is saying and why he is saying it rather than trying to remember mere details.

Research shows that most people talk at a rate of between 125-180 words per minute, but we can listen and comprehend at a rate of 600-900 words per minute, depending upon the complexity of the information being presented. This means that a listener's mind is fully utilized only approximately one-fourth to one-fifth of the time, leaving about 425-720 words per minute of spare thinking time. What do we typically do with our excess thinking time? We're apt to become bored or impatient with the relatively slow progress the speaker is making, and our thoughts turn elsewhere, occasionally darting back to the speaker. To be an effective listener, you should use your excess thought speed to your advantage.

First, analyze and interpret the information that the speaker is presenting. How can this data help you make a sale? Are his facts accurate? What could have influenced his opinions? What is he *not* saying? Next, prepare questions and appropriate responses. Without sacrificing your full attention during important periods of listening, think of follow-up questions to ask the prospect based on the direction of the sales interview. Also, if you think ahead, you can often anticipate what the prospect will ask you and can therefore prepare an appropriate response.

Finally, isolate all the main points the prospect is making, look for details that support those points, and determine the overriding message. Use feedback and summarizing to confirm with the prospect that these are the important points or issues. Then look behind the issues for supporting details. (What is causing the prospect's current problem?

How long has the problem existed? Does it need to be solved right away?) If you have been listening effectively, the overall message should become clear.

LISTENING TECHNIQUE 11:
When the Situation Gets Hot,
Keep Cool and Listen

Often there are times during or after the sale when a prospect will become annoyed, angry, antagonistic, or arrogant. This negative behavior is demonstrated by a harsh, authoritative tone of voice, aggressive body language (standing over you, hands folded across chest defensively, pointing and wagging a finger at you, contorted facial expressions), or stinging words directed at you.

There could be many reasons why a prospect acts defensive or hostile. The prospect's words can be stinging and insulting to the salesperson who is trying to listen, understand, and cooperate. Or a prospect may use words or terms that the listener misinterprets as negative, derogatory, or indecisive. In response to a salesperson's question, a prospect may reply, "Yeah, your proposal is OK." The prospect simply may not be the type of person who overflows with enthusiasm; in his vocabulary, "OK" may be high praise. But the salesperson feels let down or defensive because he has put a tremendous amount of work into the proposal. In this case, the listener misinterprets meaning and responds emotionally to it.

When we can identify our emotional triggers—the things that set us off—we can control our emotions. If you find your negative feelings suddenly emerging, ask yourself if you are responding to the prospect's words or to the facts of the situation. It's not easy, but we must discipline ourselves and not get too upset about a prospect's viewpoint until we completely hear and understand it. Otherwise, communicative efficiency drops to zero. We begin to concentrate on the damage that has been done to our ego, or we plan an embarrassing question or a snappy comeback, visualizing the prospect's discomfort at our sharp retort. It's a no-win situation, even though the listener may feel better doing so.

Here are some suggestions to help you keep cool, listen, and dissolve the negative emotions of a prospect:

1. Stop yourself before you react to an emotional speaker. Don't flare up; instead, tell yourself that responding emotionally is counterproductive to solving the problem. Let your mind rule, not your heart. Compliment yourself for maintaining composure and control.

2. Analyze why the speaker is reacting emotionally. Would you feel the same under similar conditions? What does the speaker really mean?

3. While the speaker is dumping his or her feelings onto you, listen completely. Let the prospect release his emotions. As tempting as it may be, don't jump in to disagree, give advice, criticize, or argue. Even if you have a good way to correct a sales situation that the prospect is angry about, let him finish speaking first. Only when the prospect cools down will he be rational and receptive to your comments or suggestions.

4. Never exhibit negative body language—stiffening your spine, clenching your fists, tightening your facial muscles, frowning, smirking, or crossing your arms across your chest. Maintain natural (not glaring) eye contact and a relaxed, upright sitting position.

5. When appropriate, nod and use acknowledging statements that tell the prospect that you understand how he feels, although you don't necessarily agree. "I understand how you feel," "Uh-huh," "I see," and the like show empathy without expressing agreement or disagreement.

6. Check with the prospect to make sure that you know what the problem is. You cannot solve a problem or resolve an emotional issue unless you know the details about it. Provide feedback to the prospect as to what you think his feelings are and what the real issues are. This not only shows that you have been listening, but that you're headed toward resolving the situation. One example:

> "It's important to me that I completely under-
> stand your feelings on what the specific problems
> are. As I understand it, you feel that we had
> led you to believe that our product could do
> more than it is really capable of. You also feel
> that you have not received the support after
> the sale that you were promised. Are those
> your feelings or is there something I left out?"

7. Agree with the prospect if appropriate and offer an apology if needed. If you can't agree, explain what happened or why you can't completely meet the prospect's requirements or requests. Try to reach an acceptable compromise. Put yourself in the prospect's shoes and ask yourself what you would like the salesperson to do in your case. Here are some examples:

> "Mr. Prospect, I totally agree with you. Getting
> the furniture delivered a week ago was impor-
> tant. We messed up and I'd be angry if I were
> in your shoes. No excuses, but I want to sincerely
> apologize for this problem."

> "Ms. Prospect, you're disappointed and I don't
> blame you at all. I feel personally responsible
> for this problem. I'm very sorry. I'm going to
> drop everything else this afternoon to work
> with you to get this resolved."

8. Show the prospect that you want to help out immediately. Make a specific recommendation on

how to resolve the problem and get the prospect's agreement on it. If you think the prospect will be cooperative and reasonable, ask him how *he* would like to correct the problem.

LISTENING TECHNIQUE 12:
Use Empathetic Listening

When you share a sorrow, it lessens;
when you share a joy, it increases.

RALPH WALDO EMERSON

Have you ever wondered how some people can approach total strangers and within a matter of minutes begin telling them intimate details about their lives? Professionals who deal with people problems—psychiatrists, psychologists, marriage counselors, clergy members, and the like—know that before they can help their clients solve their problems, they've got to identify what the problems are. To do so, they've got to somehow get their clients to bare their souls—to open up and freely discuss subjects that may be very sensitive. In this sense, it's similar to a sales situation. Prospects may feel embarrassed to say that they have concerns that may appear nit-picky or silly. They may feel reluctant to tell you of their tastes, real desires, or the actual reasons for buying because they consider them out of the ordinary.

When I sold computers for a major manufacturer, I had a prospect who agreed with all the major benefits of how our computer system would help him with his accounting but hesitated to make a decision. After I got his trust and showed patience with him, he finally revealed the real reason why he was holding off: he didn't like the *appearance* of the computer! He was afraid to mention what seemed like a trivial, illogical, non-businesslike reason for not buying.

One powerful technique that is used to get people to reveal their innermost opinions and feelings is empathetic listening. Empathy is described as projecting ourselves into the world of others. It's an excellent way of identifying with their thoughts, attitudes, and—most important— feelings. Many times a purchase decision is made for emotional, not logical, reasons, and that's why it's important to find out a prospect's true feelings concerning a purchase.

When people listen empathetically, they clear their minds of distractions, individual preferences, biases, and values. They concentrate their listening within their prospect's frame of reference, striving to see things from his point of view. Empathy and sympathy are different. With sympathy, you feel sorry for the person you are listening to. Very few people want pity. But when you display empathy, you feel with your prospect. It's a matter of responding equally to another's joy with joy, sadness with sadness, and concern with concern. In this way, you are truly identifying with the spirit of the other person. However, because all of us are unique, total empathy is never quite possible. We can't know exactly how the other person is feeling or the degree and complexity of that feeling, as much as we may try.

When a psychologist or counselor uses empathetic listening, he is showing sincerity, warmth, and genuine concern; therefore, he reinforces and encourages the client to talk about sensitive topics. When people self-disclose, they must be handled gently and carefully. They feel very vulnerable while they're opening up and disclosing private, deep-down feelings or secrets. Nothing is quite as soothing as empathetic listening. When a salesperson empathetically listens, he projects a message to the prospect that says, "I understand how you feel, I care, and I want to help." If used properly, empathetic listening is one of the strongest interpersonal skills that you can use to build rapport and trust with your prospects.

Selling is a knowledge game. The more information you have about your prospect and his business, the stronger your sales position is when compared to your competitor's. Your sales strategy and proposal will be much more effective because you can address his particular problems and needs more accurately and thoroughly. There are two categories of information a prospect possesses. The first is surface information about his company and its operations, organization, goals, and problems. This information is usually easy to get. It's necessary, but limited in value. Most prospects share this information with all salespeople.

The second and more important category of information is inside information, which is known only to people within that organization—usually by those who are influential in the organization. This private and sensitive information gives valuable insights about the real issues involved that can affect a sale, such as the politics of the organization, the personal motivations of the key decision-makers in the organization, and the true nuts-and-bolts factors that will get the sale. When a salesperson can obtain this inside information, he has an edge over his competitors. This information is rarely given out to just any salesperson, but it is given out to the salesperson who is liked, trusted, respected, and known to be ethical and discreet. Being an empathetic listener greatly improves your chances of getting this important information.

The best salespeople in the world do not think like salespeople; instead, they constantly try to think and feel like their prospects. In this way, they can anticipate what questions or objections a prospect may have. By using empathy, they can better understand what motivates that person and how their product can specifically fulfill the prospect's wants and desires. They can then plan how to approach the prospect, what benefits to emphasize, and how to overcome potential obstacles to the sale. The following steps will help you build your empathetic listening skills.

1. *Try to think and, most of all, feel like your prospect.* Keep an open mind and ask yourself these types of questions: I wonder how I would feel about this if I were he or she? I wonder what my prospect has gone through to feel that way? What are his personal motivations?

2. *Use mirroring techniques.* Mirroring is body language behavior that naturally and spontaneously mimics that of the person you're talking with. Mirroring often occurs spontaneously and, for the most part, goes unnoticed in everyday situations. Lovers seated at a restaurant table lean in the same direction, smile at the same time, and gesture in synchronized rhythm, or an assistant follows his boss's lead in sitting positions during a meeting. In a sales situation, if the prospect smiles, gestures a lot, and moves toward the salesperson, the salesperson smiles more, gestures more, and moves closer also. The salesperson's positive reaction reinforces and supports the prospect's actions and encourages him to continue to act friendly and open. If the prospect takes on an air of concern as shown by a subdued or tight facial expression, stiff posture, and somber tone of voice, he is indirectly but strongly saying, "Let's get serious here. This is important to me." The salesperson should mirror the prospect with a serious tone of voice and somber facial expression.

Discreet mirroring done naturally and casually puts the other person at ease. The more precise the mirroring, the greater the empathy shown and the possibility of agreement between the individuals. With mirroring, the chances are improved that the two will cooperate and move in the same direction.

However, you *don't* want to mirror a prospect who is angry at you for some problem that occurred with the sale or is indifferent about you, your company, or its products. In general, do not mirror any behavior or mood that may endanger the sale.

3. *Use supportive statements.* Use statements that demonstrate to prospects that you are encouraging them to express their feelings and that you are trying to understand those feelings. Here are some examples: "I can imagine how you felt." "That must have been tremendously frustrating." "I totally agree with you." "You have a right to feel disappointed." Another get-in-step technique that indicates that you comprehend the prospect's feelings is suggesting how you think he might feel about a concern. This encourages him to talk openly about it in order to explain, justify, or deny your comment. Here are some examples of get-in-step statements showing empathy:

Salesperson: You feel hurt.
Prospect: Darn right, I feel hurt. Let me tell you what happened.
Salesperson: You feel we should give you the added discount, even though you ordered less then the agreement stated.
Prospect: I sure do. After all we've been doing business for over five years. I think you owe it to me.

This technique is an excellent way to show concern or to get the prospect to blow off steam, which enables you to calmly address the problem later. If the prospect harbors resentment without expressing it and getting satisfaction, the sales relationship will suffer.

4. *Avoid casual remarks that show lack of concern.* The opposite of an empathetic statement is one that is impersonal, insensitive, or just awkward. Avoid such

remarks or cliches as "Ah, that happens—live and learn, I say," "I'm sure everyone feels that way," and "When you look back on it tomorrow, you'll laugh at the whole situation."

5. *Tell the prospect that it's OK to feel that way.* To get your prospects to reveal hidden concerns, use empathetic statements that encourage them to express their real feelings without having to risk embarrassment or harsh judgment. Do some initial probing and see if you can guess what is really bothering the prospect. Then explain that it's not unusual for a person to feel that way and that it's perfectly OK for him to voice his feelings, regardless of how trivial or foolish it may seem to him. For example, here is how I handled the appearance-conscious prospect I mentioned earlier: "Mr. Prospect, you're going to be using your computer in a glass-enclosed computer room that will be a showcase for your clients to see. A lot of my customers, believe it or not, are concerned about the appearance of their computer. I can understand that very well. I think it's a legitimate factor to consider."

LISTENING TECHNIQUE 13:
Listen for Vague or Incomplete Information and for Important Sales Cues

One problem that often occurs in person-to-person communication is when the speaker knows exactly what he is talking about, but the listener does not. The use of vague or relative terms is a common cause of this. Prospects frequently use terms that are perfectly clear to them, but obscure to us. As listeners, it's our job to understand the prospect's frame of reference—to clarify and get the prospect's definition of general terms such as *big, small, light, heavy, fast,* and *slow,* or subjective terms like *clean* and *attractive.* For example, a prospect may tell a salesperson that he needs a less expensive automobile than the top-of-the-line model. The salesperson, using *his* definition of less expensive, interprets this to mean about $2,000 less; the prospect, however, is thinking $4,000 less.

Size, time, distance, performance, and expense are relative terms that mean different things to different people. If these terms are important in the sales call, the salesperson should get the prospect to define or explain them immediately or later in the sales call, whichever is appropriate. Illustration 10 lists general and relative terms that are often used in both selling situations and personal ones.

There is nothing wrong in a speaker using general words, as long as his listener has the same understanding of the terms that he does. Don't leave it to chance, though. Ask the prospect what he really means by these terms. Here are examples of dialogues between prospects and salespeople:

> Prospect: I really need a photocopy machine that's compact.
> Salesperson: How small a machine in terms of size or weight do you need?
> Prospect: Your product looks good, but I need something a little less expensive.
> Salesperson: What price are you considering?
> Prospect: I guess we ought to go ahead and order some.
> Salesperson: How many would you like to order?

It's very important to listen for cues that can give you the crucial information you need to get the sale. Prospects often touch on areas that a salesperson needs to know more about; therefore, it's necessary for the salesperson to get the prospect to define vague terms, explain or justify unclear statements, expand further on points sketchily made, and give examples or illustrations to

ILLUSTRATION 10
ABSTRACT TERMS USED IN SALES SITUATIONS

Time

- right away
- promptly
- soon
- in a couple of days
- in the future
- in a little while
- as soon as possible
- shortly
- later
- after lunch
- years from now
- before you know it

Performance, operation

- fast
- difficult
- precise
- dependable
- accurate
- expandable
- transportable
- automatic
- productive
- maintenance-free
- durable
- powerful

Size, shape, weight, composition

- big
- short
- dense
- long
- sleek
- skinny
- heavy
- compact
- shiny
- small
- dense
- rigid

Measures, quantity, distance

- enough
- many
- close by
- a bit more
- marginal
- several
- ample
- minimal
- plenty
- far away
- more
- a few

Condition of product

- like new
- fair
- needs improvement
- brand new
- reconditioned
- superior
- excellent
- mint condition
- some defects
- reject
- slightly used
- original condition

Values, judgments, opinions, benefits

- good
- inexpensive
- better
- stylish
- attractive
- economical
- guaranteed
- valuable
- profitable
- worthwhile
- fool-proof
- fair

clarify problems, goals, needs, or other considerations that affect a sale.

Here are some examples showing a prospect picking up a potentially important listening cue and then getting the prospect to expand on or explain it:

> Prospect: I guess if things were a little different, we'd consider installing your machines now.
> Salesperson: A little different? In what way?

> Prospect: Yeah, we considered that approach, but found out later that it was not feasible.
> Salesperson: Hmm. Not feasible? Why is that?

LISTENING TECHNIQUE 14:
Listen for and Observe Buying Signals

Listening can take on critical importance when a prospect is sending out buying signals. If a salesperson quickly picks up on these signals, he can react to them and close the sale earlier. Studies have shown that picking up and reacting to buying signals can actually increase a salesperson's effectiveness and sales productivity 10-50 percent. Missing buying signals can unnecessarily lengthen and complicate the sale, and, worst of all, open it to the competition.

Buying signals are generated when a prospect says or does something that indicates he has a favorable opinion of your products/services/company or that the prospect is anxious to go ahead and order the product. When a prospect has gone through the mental decision-making process and has decided to buy (or is strongly leaning toward buying), he has assumed "mental ownership." As a prospect becomes more favorably inclined toward a sales proposal, he will start emitting either subconscious or intentional positive signals that can help a salesperson speed the process to a close.

An adage in selling says that if you listen carefully, the buyer will tell you when he's ready to buy, sometimes before he even knows he's decided. Buying signals vary in intensity, ranging from the prospect showing mild or increasing interest to asking, "Where do I sign?" Some buying signals are subtle and can occur early in the sales cycle. Toward the latter part of the sales cycle, buying signals usually become stronger and more direct as the prospect leans toward a decision to buy your product. It's the salesperson's responsibility to listen and watch for buying signals and then use either trial closes or an actual close.

One type of buying signal is a series of detailed, specific questions about a product or service. The more detailed the question and the more related to your product, the stronger the buying signal. It demonstrates that the prospect may know quite a bit about your product; he's done his homework and has paid close attention to you. It also indicates the prospect's interest in your product or company.

The following questions are examples of what a prospect may ask if he is interested:

—"Can I specify the color?"

—"How do you ship—by truck or rail? What is a typical delivery period? Suppose I want it sooner?"

—"What if I needed repairs in one day? Is that possible to get?"

—"What joint marketing or promotional help could I expect from your company?"

—"Do you think the AB32 model is powerful enough for my needs? How many of my people do you think should be trained to operate it?"

—"Can I keep a copy of your sales agreement to show my lawyers?"

—"Can I return it in a week if it doesn't do the job?"

There's another category of questions to listen for called noncommittal questions. Here, a prospect pre-empts a question with a noncommittal phrase designed to give the salesperson the impression that he has not made up his mind (even if he has). The reason that some prospects do this is to avoid being pushed by the salesperson or to hold out for a better negotiating position on the sales agreement. Here are some examples of these "teaser" questions that usually indicate buying interest:

—"We haven't decided yet, but let me ask you this...?"

—"It's not important, but just out of curiosity, I was wondering if...?"

—"In case I happen to decide to buy, I'd like to know if...?"

—"Oh, by the way, can your company...?"

Other noncommittal inquiries are conditional questions; they begin with words like *assuming, suppose, if,* and *let's say.* Here are some examples:

—"Assuming that we were interested in your proposal...?"

—"Suppose for a moment we selected your company for this project...?"

—"If we did go ahead and buy from you...?"

—"Let's say that we were interested in your leasing agreement...?"

Another major category of buying signals to listen for is strong, optimistic statements that indicate a prospect is getting closer to making a buying decision. Pay attention to this type of buying signal: It is 99 percent accurate. It relates to your product exclusively and implies that the prospect has made up his mind and is now simply focusing on the minor follow-up details of the purchase. Notice how these statements made by the prospect demonstrate "mental ownership":

—"I definitely want the blue seats. They will look great with the light-blue exterior of the car."

—"I want to wrap this deal up by Friday. I'd like to get our contracts people together with you as soon as possible."

—"That feature is really nice. I like that and so will the operators using the machine."

—"I've got to get the vice-president of manufacturing to see this proposal. He'll love it."

Besides verbal clues, another type of buying signal to watch for is body language and behavior. When a salesperson first begins to work with a new prospect, the prospect usually tends to be aloof, guarded, or formal. However, some selling situations, like retail selling, require a quick-sale technique, and it can be difficult to nurture rapport in such a short time period. Changes in body language and behavior can occur quickly in a prospect if he is close to making a buying decision. These physical characteristics indicate that a buyer has made up his mind to buy from you:

• He becomes more friendly. The air of coolness disappears and is replaced by approving nods and frequent smiling. He may joke or laugh more easily with the salesperson. His body may lean toward the salesperson or, if standing, move closer. Natural eye contact with the salesperson may become stronger, his tone of voice may become softer, and he may use the salesperson's name more frequently.

• He is less defensive. He mentions fewer objections or tough questions and accepts your sales presentation points. He becomes more willing to compromise and offers to negotiate reasonably.

• He becomes cooperative by sharing information and personal feelings. He expresses general enthusiasm for the salesperson's product or service.

● His personal sense of burden over making a decision is lifted. This is reflected in more relaxed facial expressions and posture, animated gestures, and signs of relaxation such as unbuttoning his jacket and lighting a cigarette.

● He may carefully look at your sales agreement again as if to feel completely comfortable with it prior to "taking the plunge."

● He may carefully examine the product again as if looking for something wrong with it. This is a way for a prospect to justify the purchase further by saying to himself, "Well, I checked it over very carefully for problems or faults, and I didn't find any." The prospect may also handle or look at the product in a very thoughtful or possessive way that gives the impression that he is envisioning using it in his business.

● He may take out some paper, a pen, and a calculator to check your quotation figures, his cost estimates or budget, or other important figures related to buying.

Remember that one of these actions alone may not be a strong buying signal, but when several are combined, they become more meaningful predictors of the mood swing and attitude change that indicates greater buying interest.

See the chapter on sample questions for examples of trial closes and closes to use when you detect conclusive buying signals.

5

Reading Nonverbal Signals

There was speech in their dumbness,
language in their very gesture.

WILLIAM SHAKESPEARE

The Winter's Tale

Everything that a person says and does ultimately affects the meaning and outcome of communication. So far I have primarily focused on the spoken word. Yet words form only part of the overall meaning of a message. We communicate with more than just words. Anyone who has seen a good mime, an accomplished actor, a baseball coach giving signals to his team, or a sign language interpreter knows that there are other powerful ways of getting points across. Researchers have long recognized that there are three basic components of interpersonal communication: the spoken word, tone of voice, and nonverbal actions, or body language.

Illustration 11 shows these components and three other elements that create an overall personal impression of a person and add nuances to the meaning of a message being communicated. The message meaning being transmitted from the person you're speaking with is a sort of bull's-eye—something you should aim for. Directly surrounding and having the most direct influence on the meaning of the message are the three components—the spoken word, tone of voice, and body language. The outer segment of the circle, farther away from the message

ILLUSTRATION 11
MESSAGE MEANING AND OVERALL IMPRESSION

SPOKEN WORD
(structured language)

- Words used for specific meanings
- Combined into logical sentences
- Most commonly used and accepted
  form of communicating
- Crucial for facts-oriented messages

BODY LANGUAGE
(action language)

- Gestures   • Posture
- Body movement   • Facial expressions
- Position and distance
- Body language is often done
  unconsciously and difficult to suppress

VOICE TONE
(mood language)

- Part of personality and voice makeup
- Gives shades of meaning to spoken word
- Often works together with body language

DRESS/GROOMING
(appearance langauge)

- Clothes (tailoring, quality)
- Jewelry   • Hairstyles   • Hygiene
- Fragrances   • Makeup
- Accessories (attache case, pocketbook, etc.)
- Dress/grooming shows a person's "package"

POSSESSIONS
(object language)

Display of material things such as:

- Homes   • Cars   • Boats
- Furniture   • Art objects
- Audio/video systems

AFFILIATIONS/ACTIVITIES
(lifestyle language)

- Sports   • Hobbies
- Clubs/associations
- Political affiliations
- Leisure activities

COMBINED, THESE COMMUNICATE:		
IDEAS	VALUES	MOTIVATIONS
FEELINGS	PRINCIPLES	ASPIRATIONS
NEEDS	SELF-CONCEPTS	ATTITUDES

meaning, consists of those elements (dress/grooming, possessions, affiliations/activities) that have an indirect influence on what the message really is.

Body language or kinesics is the study of communication through body movements, facial expressions, posture, gestures, and position with regard to other people. Depending upon the type of communication, the spoken word can actually take a back seat to unspoken aspects. Anthropologist Ray Birdwhistell, a respected authority and one of the first researchers on modern nonverbal communication, has estimated that in a typical two-person conversation, the spoken message conveys less than 35 percent of the total meaning of the message; the remaining 65 percent of the message is communicated by unspoken factors. In his book *Silent Messages,* Dr. Albert Mehrabian, a professor of psychology at UCLA, states that feelings and attitudes are expressed 7 percent by words, 38 percent by tone of voice, and 55 percent by nonverbal actions. This study pointed out the significance that voice tone and body language have in expressing feelings and attitudes—93 percent of a message is actually communicated without words! In this case, "actions speak louder than words." Now, on the other hand, if a speaker is giving a facts-oriented presentation, for example, on a technical, scientific, business, or financial topic, word meanings (spoken word) would be the main component contributing to the actual meaning of the overall message. The percentages may vary, but most researchers agree that nonverbal communication is by far the most influential component in everyday interpersonal communication. Yet most of us know very little about it.

Body language is almost always done subconsciously and, since it is triggered by emotions, is very difficult for people to suppress and control. Hence, it tends to be spontaneous in nature, and the stronger the emotions, the more body language displayed.

Body language plays a major part in interpersonal relations, especially when you first meet someone. We react to people, not just to sterile ideas, facts, concepts, or principles. Maybe that's why businesspeople fly great distances to conduct and close important business deals in person rather than on the telephone. Most of us feel that it's easier and more effective to influence another and to exert our prestige, expertise, or power when we see another person face-to-face.

The study of body language has come a long way, but it is still a relatively new and evolving science. Unfortunately, there is no cohesive theory of nonverbal communication. Although there are a large number of scientific papers that cover specific areas of nonverbal research, the studies and results are not unified into a single, all-encompassing theory. We presently know more about how people react than we do about why they react.

Benefits

Learning to watch carefully for body language signals can benefit you in your job and in your personal life. Nonverbal clues can give out a tremendous amount of information about a person and can aid you in developing a keener sensitivity in your relationships with others. If you're able to detect and interpret signals from others and then send your own appropriate messages, you can better maintain control in interpersonal relationships, discussions, negotiations, and sales calls.

If through body language you know what mental and emotional state other people are in, you can respond appropriately to them in order to bring about the results you want. Body language signals from others can tell you when to change your approach and how to change it—

e.g., when and how to change your sales call tactics, your presentation agenda, or your personal style. This could mean talking about something different, adjusting *your* nonverbal behavior, presenting more convincing proof of your product claims, or using other techniques to meet your selling objectives. To cite a common example, body language feedback can alert you to how well a person understands what you are saying. When you see a stymied look or a blank stare, you can be reasonably certain that the person has lost the thread of the conversation. So you stop momentarily and either ask if the person understands or repeat an earlier point in terms that are more digestible.

Perceptive salespeople know that nonverbal signals often can influence a sale more significantly than just spoken words. As salespeople become more experienced in reading body language, they will make quicker and easier sales. Gerhard Gschwandtner Associates of Falmouth, Virginia, conducts training courses in how to read prospects' body language. This training cleverly simplifies reading body language by categorizing it into three types of traffic light signals:

● Green light signals show that the prospect is open, positive, and receptive. A salesperson then should continue his sales dialogue or presentation with the same pace and direction. Green means "full speed ahead."

● Yellow light signals indicate that the salesperson is probably losing the prospect's interest. The salesperson should change tactics to instill added interest and to resolve any questions or minor concerns a prospect has. Yellow means "caution."

● Red light signals show that the prospect is actually resistant to what is being said or done in the sales process. These negative body language signals tell the salesperson to stop and find out the source of resistance to the sale and then strongly redirect his sales tactics to attempt to recover a sale that is close to being lost. Red means "danger" and "stop."

Gschwandtner Associates figures show that the average sales increase for firms that conduct training courses in body language is 41 percent. Of course, to be effective, nonverbal communication skills, like other listening skills, have to be practiced and refined constantly.

Look for the "Big Picture"

When nonverbal communication was first being recognized and studied, some enthusiastic researchers tried to interpret the meanings of individual gestures and body movements. For example, they established that when a person crosses his arms over his chest, this is a defensive gesture. But is it always? Many of us occasionally use this gesture simply because it feels comfortable. But suppose a person first crosses his arms over his chest, then pulls away from you, displays a rigid posture, and shows a tense facial expression. These several related body actions when joined together indicate that he is uncomfortable or upset over something that you have said or done.

Understanding and accurately interpreting individual gestures and other body signals in isolation (separated from their context) is very difficult and will often yield false readings on your part. It's been estimated by some body language experts that there are over 5,000 possible hand gestures and over 20,000 possible facial expressions. Can you imagine cataloging and attaching a specific meaning to each of those? And this does not even include posture or other body movements.

The key to reading and analyzing body language correctly is to add up all the elements, thus arriving at a composite, complete meaning—the "big picture." Each hand gesture, body movement, and facial expression is like a word in a language: one must structure the words into logical sentences to express complete, meaningful thoughts. Watch for a pattern of actions that, when linked together, can more accurately reflect a person's true feelings, attitudes, and message. One body position or movement could mean any number of things, or it could have no meaning at all. It's the total cluster of actions that spells out the overall body language message.

Nonverbal signals can also reinforce or contradict the spoken word. Verbal and nonverbal behavior can communicate conflicting messages. A typical example is when your spouse, friend, boss, or co-worker says, "I am *not* angry!" His enraged tone of voice and hostile, rigid body language strongly say otherwise. Or consider a lover saying, "I hate you—I never want to see you again" with reluctance and slight hesitation. The longing eyes and forward lean of the body silently shout, "Don't leave. You hurt me. Let's talk."

When body language goes against the spoken word, the general rule is to accept the nonverbal cues and discount the words. This is because body language is reflexive in nature and is very hard to fake, unless a person has had proper training and maintains constant vigilance and strong self-control. Nonverbal behavior can also add strength to the spoken word, giving emphasis to it. It can give the verbal aspect that needed punch. For example, a salesperson rebuffed by a tough prospect who complains about spending money replies, "I understand your concern about keeping expenses down. Yet you agree that our product can give you a return on your investment of between 35 and 43 percent, and that's 15 percent higher than your corporate guidelines. We can help your department with our product!" The words are accompanied and reinforced by strong eye contact, confident gestures and posture, and a sincere, trustworthy tone of voice. In this case, body language and the spoken word work together to boost the effect of the overall meaning of the message.

Categorizing nonverbal signals into several major areas can make it easier to interpret them and therefore see the "big picture" first before delving deeper into the real meaning. These categories are open and closed gestures and positions, physical distance from others, and position in relation to others.

Open Vs. Closed Positions

Open body language shows positive thoughts and feelings. When a person displays openness, he is at peace with himself, relaxed, receptive, trusting, cooperative, or happy. Open body positions and actions indicate that a person is willing to listen and will most likely be agreeable to the discussion and the person he is dealing with. Open body positions displayed by a prospect tell a salesperson that he is on the right track with his sales approach and dialogue and that he is heading closer to the sale. If the prospect continues to react in such a positive manner, the sale will probably be assured. The term *open* is used because people exhibiting this type of body language "open up," literally and figuratively. Their arms may be outstretched and open, relaxed and free to gesture. Their posture and body movements tend to be loose, showing casualness and smooth motion. Their legs are not locked together but instead are comfortably placed next to each other or slightly spread apart. Their facial expression is receptive, calm, or happy. A complete air of openness is communicated by a person using open body gestures, which encourages other people to approach him freely. In this personal state, people are almost always receptive to your ideas, suggestions, and sales presentation.

The category of closed body positions and gestures consists of those in which people tend to withdraw into themselves, back off, tighten up, or prepare to go on the offensive. Some researchers consider a combination of withdrawal-type closed body gestures a publicly expressed form of a fetal position. Examples of actions that people use to close their bodies include folding the arms tightly across the chest (as if to shield themselves against harm or create self-comfort), placing the hands over the mouth, crossing the legs and putting them into a tightly locked position, and projecting a tense, controlled, or blank facial expression. These closed body positions say "I'm not comfortable with you, with what you're saying, or what is happening here. I'm not openly listening and accepting what you are saying. You can't get through to me."

Closed positions and gestures indicate that a person is experiencing some kind of emotional turmoil—perhaps feeling threatened, nervous, afraid, ignored, offended, guarded, defensive, antagonistic, skeptical, confused, or any other negative or uncomfortable emotion. When a person experiences emotional distress, he will withdraw silently (repressing strong feelings), or display some sort of defensive or hostile behavior toward others. Closed positions are a barometer of these feelings. They indicate definite roadblocks to acceptance. Getting a sale while a person harbors such feelings and displays such mannerisms is highly unlikely. When a person is showing closed body language, we must find out the source of his negative emotions and deal with them adequately in order to get the prospect in a positive, cooperative frame of mind.

Distance and Direction

Another general category of body language deals with the distance and physical position people use when relating to each other. These two broad factors can indicate how a person is feeling toward and reacting to other people. For example, researchers agree that making an effort to move closer to you (except when attempting to dominate you through aggressive behavior) is a friendly overture indicating that a person is interested in you or what you are saying. When people suddenly move away or maintain what seems to be an unnatural distance between you, they may be signaling that they want to keep you at arm's length; something is separating you, and not just in terms of distance.

The direction of a person's body in relation to yours can give you a clue as to whether that person is receptive and friendly toward you or the conversation or is bored or negatively inclined in some respect. A person who turns his whole body away from you when talking to you is saying nonverbally, "I don't want to be part of this." If closed gestures are added to increased distance and direction away from you, the negative message becomes stronger. Turning away means exclusion. You'll often see a person in a business meeting sitting farther away from the conference table than the rest of the group, perhaps even facing an exit door instead of the other participants. By moving back and facing away from others, that person has actively separated himself (physically) and his thoughts and feelings (mentally and emotionally) from the rest of the group. When a person makes a concerted effort to face another person, and other positive body language signs are present, this indicates a sincere desire to listen to and get to know the other person better. Swiveling the upper body toward another and aligning the shoulders parallel to that person shows rapport being developed. On the other hand, moving very close to someone and facing him directly can be a provocative, challenging gesture caused by mutual anger or intimidation. In this case, other belligerent gestures such as finger pointing, rigid body posture, and angry facial expressions are usually present.

Other Nonverbal Factors

Another important aspect of listening with your eyes is evaluating your prospect's possessions and surroundings. In a business environment, the decor and contents of a person's office can give you a good clue as to what type of individual you are dealing with. Experts who study human behavior agree that many people attempt to make statements to other people with the possessions they have. Keeping up with the Joneses (or bettering them) can mean driving a certain brand of imported automobile, having a fancy home in a posh neighborhood, belonging to an exclusive country club, or wearing $800 custom-tailored suits. People design these possessions and lifestyles consciously or subconsciously to create a desirable image of themselves and to project that image to others they come into contact with. On the other hand, some people use apathy, neglect, or nonconformist behavior to exhibit certain negative traits or self-images to the world. Their possessions or surroundings make a counter-impressive statement about them.

A person's business office can give valuable clues to his personality, tastes, values, hobbies, activities, ideas, and motivations. Listening with your eyes—carefully observing a person's office and possessions—can help you to size up your prospect better, thus enabling you to create a customized sales strategy and presentation that will effectively focus on the prospect's personal needs and desires. While you are in your prospect's office, look around. Observe everything you can about it in a subtle way. Then try to piece together what the office, its furnishings, and its other contents can tell you about your prospect. Remember, though, that your primary goal is to concentrate on listening to your prospect; don't be drawn off course by staring around the office. You'll have plenty of time to glance around when your prospect talks about areas of lesser importance to you.

A large, imposing office can indicate a prospect's personal importance. Look at how the office is decorated and furnished. Is it modern, traditional, colonial? Is the furniture of quality taste and construction? Are there many plants in the office? Is the room meticulously arranged and organized? Maybe it's stark or in disarray with papers all over the place. What kind of books and magazines are placed around? Does the prospect proudly display trophies, awards, and diplomas? Are paintings, photographs, and sculptures prominently displayed, or are slogans and commercial posters the primary decoration? See if there are any signs that your competitors have been around. Perhaps there are manuals, brochures, photographs, or gifts (customized pens, coffee mugs, clocks) that a competing salesperson left with your prospect.

Just by observing and evaluating the size, decoration, furnishings, and organization of your prospect's office, try to create a personal profile of your prospect that may tell you whether he is:

- family-oriented
- non-conformist
- people-oriented
- sloppy
- sophisticated
- competitive
- time-conscious

- recreation-oriented
- nostalgic
- meticulous
- conservative
- scholarly
- money-conscious
- immature

Reading Nonverbal Signals

Detecting and analyzing body language is a learning process, like developing any other listening skill. Some people think of it as becoming fluent in another language.

It's important for salespeople not only to recognize and be able to decipher the prospect's body language, but to use it correctly themselves. Salespeople embody as well as speak their company's message and project its image. A professional salesperson, then, in addition to delivering his · product or service message becomes the message itself. Words alone cannot close sales. *Sell yourself first, then sell your company, and your product will be easier to sell.* Therefore, it's important for you to maintain a constant vigil on your own body language. You want to be aware of potentially dangerous signals (impatience, condescension, apathy, insincerity) that you might inadvertently give out that would negatively affect your prospect and the sales outcome. You also want to plan your gestures and other actions to reinforce your words or counteract your prospect's hostile, indifferent, or otherwise counterproductive feelings.

To get started toward listening with your eyes, I recommend that you begin to study people. Watch people in a variety of business and social situations: dealing with their bosses, peers, subordinates, friends, spouse, and others. See if you can sense what is happening—how people are reacting to one another, what their feelings are toward each other, what they are talking about, and what the situation is in general. Anywhere people gather can be an excellent "reading ground." Accurately reading body language and other nonverbal information (appearance, dress, possessions) can be a tremendous benefit to you in your business career and in your personal life as well. Besides, people-watching is fun!

To help you get started, the following pages discuss clusters of nonverbal signals that can generally indicate what a person's mood and mental state are. In addition, I have included some tactics for you to use in reacting to a prospect's body language. Please keep in mind that the brief guidelines that follow are only designed to get you started and should not be thought of as an exact system that will enable you to read someone's mind. Even body language experts would not attempt that amazing feat.

Positive Signals:
Cooperation, Enthusiasm, Agreement

The body language signals that are most appreciated by a salesperson are those positive signs that show a prospect to be friendly, receptive, trusting, interested, and therefore willing to seriously consider purchasing the product or service. It's a pleasure for a salesperson to deal with a prospect who is open-minded and willing to listen eagerly to his sales presentation and accept his recommendations. It certainly is a good feeling for salespeople to be treated with respect and friendliness, since we are taught and prepared to experience resistance and rejection.

Typically, prospects exhibit positive body language signals at the end of the sales cycle, after they have established rapport with the salesperson and the salesperson has demonstrated credibility with the prospect. Positive body signals that show increased buying interest also surface after a salesperson gives a good sales presentation, mentions something about the product that really stirs the prospect's interest, or effectively answers the prospect's objections, questions, or requests. If positive signals from the prospect continue and build in intensity, there is an excellent chance that a sale will come out of it. The following clues give some additional buying signals and show other positive body language signs.

● Smiling, nodding (especially a slow, exaggerated nod), or other animated and positive facial expressions. The face appears relaxed, alert, or enthusiastic.

● Sitting on the edge of a chair with the upper body leaning eagerly forward as if straining to hear every word from the salesperson. The legs and feet are usually drawn under the chair on tiptoes. This position is commonly exhibited when a prospect is ready to sign, to compromise, or otherwise cooperate with the salesperson. It's a sign of heightened physical and psychological alertness that indicates readiness for some sort of action and is, therefore, commonly referred to as the "sprinter's position."

● Riveting (but not intimidating) eye contact that indicates intense interest in the other person and usually in what he is saying. Strong eye contact on a product while it is being exhibited or demonstrated is a good sign. Also, when a person is positively excited by something he sees, the pupils of his eyes actually dilate (open up).

● Full attention given to the salesperson; no doodling, looking at watch, or other restless behavior.

● Open body position displayed: hands rest comfortably on table or gesture in a friendly, conversational way; legs are suddenly uncrossed or feet unlocked; arms are removed from across the chest; and other loosening-up gestures are displayed, indicating that the person has just favorably changed his mind.

● Tone of voice becoming gentler and more conciliatory or more animated and enthusiastic.

● Jacket unbuttoned or removed during the discussion, or sleeves rolled up (showing informality). The opening of a coat can signal an opening-up to you and your ideas or recommendations.

● Slightly tilted head. You see dogs doing this when they listen intently. This gesture usually indicates a deep receptiveness to what is being said.

● Rubbing palms together slowly as if to say, "Ah, that sounds really good to me. I can't wait to buy it!" It's a sign of anticipating something good that's about to happen.

● Touching, grabbing, or patting a person on the arm, elbow, shoulder, or back. This can show warmth, friendship, concern, or sympathy. It can indicate that the toucher feels comfortable with us. Please be aware, though, that touching can carry a strong emotional (and sometimes sexual) message, and if done too early or in a business environment between a man and woman, it can be misconstrued as insincere or pushy and therefore un-appreciated.

● Moving physically closer to another. This can be viewed as a warming-up gesture. A sudden pulling away can spell trouble.

● Standing up with both feet spread apart and hands on hips. This can illustrate a sense of readiness to act or even a feeling of urgency. This display of mental and physical readiness can transmit this message in a sales situation: "Well, let's get going. Give me the sales contract to sign already, will you?"

Responding to Positive Signals

—If your prospect compliments you, your company, or its product, show appreciation by thanking the prospect. This can help to reinforce him to continue saying positive things.

—Continue your sales strategy and dialogue in the same direction if the prospect seems to be positively excited. Obviously, you've hit his "hot" buttons.

—Listen intently to encourage the prospect to cooperate further with you and display other positive signs of friendliness and sales interest.

—If your prospect is enthusiastic and excited about your product, reflect that enthusiasm yourself to keep momentum building. Keep your focus on the key benefits of your product that interest the prospect. Assure him that he is definitely making the right decision by continuing the evaluation process and seriously considering buying your product.

—Continue to use open body gestures and move closer to the prospect if he is warming up to you.

Thinking Signals:
Evaluation, Reflection, Hesitation

A salesperson's ultimate goal, of course, is to close the sale. But before a prospect signs on the dotted line, he must first understand what the salesperson's product or service is, what it does, and how it can help him in his business or personal life. Then, before he is motivated to make an actual buying decision, he must agree with the major aspects of a salesperson's proposal or sales presentation. If a prospect is intrigued with a salesperson's product, he will go through a mental process of analyzing and evaluating the sales situation. A prospect, in trying to reach a decision one way or the other, will almost always exhibit certain body language gestures as he actively listens and carefully thinks about going ahead with the purchase.

During this mental (and many times emotional) evaluation process, a prospect is often hesitant and uncertain about making a buying decision, especially if it's an important, expensive purchase. He may change the course of his potential decision several times, even within a short period of time during a sales call, before making a firm, committed decision. This is a purposeful procrastination, a time to pause for thought. This pensiveness can be shown by the following types of nonverbal and verbal clues.

● Repeated hair-twisting, mustache-smoothing, stroking of beard, scratching.

● Doodling that slowly, deliberately, and repeatedly retraces one design.

● Assuming a meditative, concentrating appearance: hands clasped behind the back, head down, shoulders bent, and eyes downcast.

- Intense gaze or blank stare, usually out a window or at the floor, wall, or ceiling, accompanied by a wrinkled forehead and motionless head.

- Putting earpiece of eyeglasses in the mouth. Slowly and deliberately removing eyeglasses and methodically wiping the lenses, even if they don't need it. This pausing-for-thought gesture may be done several times, as if to say "I've got to see this decision in a clearer fashion."

- With head bent over and eyes closed, pinching the bridge of the nose, rubbing the lips, or resting the forehead in one hand. This cluster can indicate deep thought and concern about the upcoming decision.

- Chin in the palm of the hand with the thumb on one cheek and the remaining fingers wrapped around the other cheek. This may be accompanied by a slow stroking of the chin. The prospect may sit forward in his chair while doing this.

- Repeating something like "Hmm" several times to himself.

- Asking confirming questions to reassure himself that he is making the right decision ("You definitely can commit to getting those machines delivered by the 15th, right?").

Responding to Thinking Signals

—Don't interrupt the person who is thinking. Let him naturally and comfortably decide whether or not to buy your product. Interrupting a person can be disruptive or considered rude and can cause the prospect to lose his train of thought. If the prospect is leaning toward the sale, you may curtail this momentum by interrupting; if the prospect is going away from the sale, let him fully organize his thoughts so you can respond to them gently all at once, thus making for a quicker sale. A silence period honored by a salesperson is greatly appreciated by a prospect. Prospects really need room to breathe. Low-pressure, but professional, selling means giving a person the full opportunity to think things out before responding to you. The prospect may then say something positive, ask questions, bring up concerns, or bring forth new requirements.

—If the prospect seems to be wavering—hesitating to make a buying decision—find out why. Determine the specific reasons why your prospect is reluctant either to continue the sales dialogue or to actually buy your product now.

—Summarize all the major benefits that your product or service can offer. Show the unique qualities and strengths that your product has over its competition. Emphasize the proven results that satisfied customers have received from your product. If you can comfortably justify it, stress that your product or service offers low risk and excellent investment opportunity. People are often afraid to make a decision that could backfire on them later on.

—Anticipate and adequately deal with any questions, requests, or objections that a prospect may bring up after going through this uninterrupted thought process.

—Reassure your prospect that deciding on your product is a good decision. Use proof sources (statistics, test results, demonstrations, guarantees) to reinforce his present interest or resurface his waning desire for your product. He needs to feel, not just know, that he is about to make the right decision.

Cool Signals:
Disinterest, Restlessness, Fatigue

A prospect may be bored or disinterested for a variety of reasons. He may feel that the salesperson is boring or rambling on and on, or that the topic being discussed is unimportant to him. He may also be tired as a result of a heavy work schedule or the aftereffects of a heavy meal and drinks. Prospects typically become restless when sitting for extended periods of time listening to a comprehensive sales presentation that lasts several hours. In most cases, though, a prospect is disinterested or bored because he does not see a clear need to buy a product or service. Unfortunately, too many salespeople bombard prospects with meaningless details about their product or cover information that the prospects have heard before. Or, if a prospect hears an obviously canned pitch, he will tune out or become restless. Here are some body language and other indicators showing disinterest, restlessness, or fatigue.

● Fidgeting in seat.

● Avoiding direct eye contact with the salesperson; instead, gazing around the room, at other people in the area, at an exit door, or out the window in an attempt to find something interesting to look at. The most obvious giveaway signal is the blank, zombie-like gaze that looks like the person is asleep with his eyes open.

● Within a group, passing notes around, holding side conversations that appear to have nothing to do with the sales presentation, or telling jokes to each other.

● Lack of questions, comments, or requests from the prospect, thus showing disinterest.

● Restless gestures such as feet tapping on the floor, fingers drumming on the table, hands or fingers slapping against parts of the body, or ball-point pens clicking.

● Doodling, cleaning fingernails, frequently looking at watch.

● Repeated yawning.

● Body and head turned away from the salesperson.

● Legs crossed with one foot rapidly jiggling or moving in a broader kicking fashion.

• Prolonged reading of something (literature, visual aids, agenda) instead of concentrating on the speaker. Rereading the same information over and over is a way to keep the mind occupied.

• Head and eyelids drooping with the chin resting in one or both hands as if it were a heavy burden, or body slouched in the seat with feet and legs stretched out in front (this cluster is usually a blatant way to express feelings of sheer boredom or exhaustion).

• Frequent nodding of the head and remarks such as "Uh huh" made in a staccato fashion to hasten the discussion along and bring the sales call to a close.

Responding to Cool Signals

—Get your prospect more involved in the sales discussion. Ask relevant questions and use good listening skills to encourage the prospect to participate directly in the buying process. If you're giving a product demonstration, let your prospect operate, handle, or touch the product when appropriate. The more a person's senses are involved in an activity, the more alert and interested he becomes.

—Concentrate on discussing areas of specific interest to the prospect and cut short topics that your prospect is not concerned with. Talk about how your product or service can benefit him by solving his problems, meeting his goals, and fulfilling important personal needs and wants.

—Use relevant and interesting statistics, analogies, test reports, and product demonstrations to keep the prospect's delicate interest. Use success stories about customers who have successfully used your product. Elaborate on how the product has helped other businesses, and paint a clear picture of how those same benefits could be realized by your prospect.

—Stay away from monologues about uninteresting features, details, or technical jargon about your product unless your prospect directly or indirectly requests such information.

—Put some extra pizzazz in your speech delivery; put enthusiasm in your sales talk and avoid a monotone.

—If you're giving a group sales presentation and the prospects are showing collective signs of fatigue or restlessness, give them a break to rekindle their attention and energy.

Confident Signals: Poise, Superiority

When a person is confident, poised, and comfortable, it can show a number of things: that he is self-controlled or feels good about himself as a person, his ability to do his job, and his expertise on the subject being discussed. Strong confidence or cockiness may indicate that the prospect feels that he has the upper hand in negotiating a better sales contract with you or knows more about your type of product or service than you think he does. These body language signals also show the strength of a person's conviction or determination to get his point across or requests honored. Here are some indicators that can display confidence or even superiority.

● Strong erect sitting or standing position; no stooping or slouching in chair.

● Relatively slow (or slower than usual) rate of speech and a relaxed, lower pitch of voice.

● Frequent, direct eye contact, often accompanied by less blinking.

● Sitting back in the chair with feet on the desk and hands joined at the back of the head. This is a strong indication of a feeling of superiority or smugness.

● Joining of fingertips into the gesture commonly called "steepling" (resembling a church steeple). This gesture communicates that a person is sure of what he is saying. It can also sometimes reflect feelings of egotism or pride. The consensus of body language researchers is that the higher a person holds his hands while steepling, the more impressed he is with himself. An example of extreme steepling is when a person holds his hands formed in a steeple up to his eyes and then peers through them. This can strongly indicate that he feels dominant, more important, more knowledgeable, or otherwise superior in negotiation. The lower the steeple (e.g., in the lap), the less the superiority complex is projected.

• Facial expression shows poise, inner calm, and an overall relaxed state.

• Lack of nervous mannerisms or gestures.

Responding to Confident Signals

—Act confident and poised yourself; avoid nervous mannerisms. Smiling, a relaxed sitting position, open gestures, a slow speech rate, and lower voice pitch can project confidence.

—Don't let a prospect with a smug or superior attitude intimidate you. Remind yourself that, as a salesperson, you have a valuable service to offer and that you can help the prospect.

—Don't try to challenge or otherwise blatantly defend your position with a prospect who comes across as a know-it-all. Approach differences of opinion with a confident and calm manner that suggests professionalism.

—Get on the prospect's side by acknowledging (and, if appropriate, complimenting) his experience with or knowledge of the sales subject you are discussing.

—Analyze the perceived confidence of your prospect. Does he really believe or know something as strongly or thoroughly as you think he does, or is he simply playing a part? Proper questioning techniques can reveal the real situation.

—Subtly reveal your knowledge of and experience with the topic being discussed in a way that clearly establishes your credibility while not coming across in a bragging or otherwise offensive way.

Skeptical Signals: Doubt, Distrust, Disbelief, Confusion

Salespeople are often told in training courses to generate interest in a prospect by coming up with attention-grabbing claims (benefits) about their product or service. These claims should then be backed up by appropriate explanation and justification. For example, a salesperson tells a prospect that his machine tool has an average operating reliability (benefit) rating of 98.2 percent based on a two-year study made among users. The prospect, based on his experience using older but similar machines, feels that the figure given by the salesperson is inflated and unrealistic. The result is a negative feeling—a distrusting attitude. The salesperson's point comes across as far-fetched and hard to believe, even though it is perfectly true.

This suspicion, doubt, or rejection is then evidenced by body language signals that are usually loud and clear: "I'm not buying what you are saying, so I'm not buying your product or service." The prospect needs more reassurance and proof that the salesperson's claim is true, so the salesperson tries to convince him. Here are some body language signals that typically show doubt and suspicion.

• Frowns, smirks, or shaking head side-to-side with mouth open showing disbelief, amazement, or "facial sarcasm."

• Raised eyebrows, sideways glances.

● Slightly open mouth with finger placed on lower teeth, accompanied by perplexed look.

● Dropping eyeglasses to lower part of nose and peering over them with head tilted downward or up at ceiling as if to say, "You've got to be putting me on. How can you say that? Do you think I'm naive?"

● Rubbing nose, playing with mustache, scratching back of head.

● Pushing back in chair and defensively crossing arms over chest.

● Within a group, sudden animated remarks made between people seated next to each other, seemingly rebuking what the salesperson has just said.

Responding to Skeptical Signals

—Empathize with your prospect. This will help you find out why your prospect doubts what you have said. Ask him about his specific doubts or confusion. Determine what it will take for your prospect to believe you fully.

—Make sure that you fully explain the point you are making. Use illustrations, examples, analogies, definitions, and explanations to enable your prospect to understand you completely. Before someone agrees with you, he must understand the issues involved.

—Provide ample proof of your statements or claims. The proof should be reliable, unbiased, and respected by the prospect. Your proof may be test results, statistics, reports from independent organizations, product demonstrations, contractual guarantees or warranties, or verification of claims from satisfied users of your product or service. This will make it easier for your prospect to agree with your points.

—Use open body positions, a calm reassuring tone of

voice, and a moderate speech rate to project sincerity and confidence.

Negative Signals:
Hostility, Anger, Frustration

There are sales situations that can, unfortunately, cause anger, argument, disappointment, defensiveness, aggressiveness, or other types of hostile behavior in a prospect. It may happen if the salesperson failed to make good on a promised previous commitment that is important to the prospect, if the salesperson directly disagrees and challenges the prospect about something (forcing the prospect to save face), or if the salesperson was negligent regarding the product order or its installation, causing considerable inconvenience to the prospect. It may be caused by some discourtesy or indiscretion on the part of the salesperson such as showing up late for a meeting or divulging confidential information to others. A prospect may be frustrated because he cannot get the salesperson to give him certain concessions (lower price, faster delivery) that he deems reasonable. Then again, a prospect's aggressiveness may have nothing to do with the salesperson at all. The prospect might just be having a completely miserable day and want to take it out on anyone he can.

A prospect will not always burst forth with obvious displays when he is angry. Sometimes, perhaps to maintain his status and personal dignity, he attempts to control his strong feelings inwardly. His voice may seem calm and his words may not be cutting, sarcastic, or challenging, but his body actions will usually reveal his true internal turmoil. If a person is angry with his boss, for example, or is in a no-win situation where he cannot or should not vent his anger without great damage to himself, he will most likely withdraw into himself and bottle up his resentment for a long time afterwards. Here are some typical nonverbal signals that display anger, frustration, or other forms of displeasure.

• Dramatically increased eye contact in a challenging, show-down way. Dilated pupils showing irritation and arousal.

• Closed body language such as hands tightly clenched on the table or lap or clutching sides of chair. Hands may be tightly locked behind the back when standing. Locked ankles may accompany other gestures. These and perhaps the palm at the back of the neck (a well-known containing gesture) indicate a holding back of deep, real emotions caused by pressure and strain such as frustration.

• Repeated scratching of nose, back of head, neck, or cheek, suggesting annoyance.

• Abrupt, aggressive body shifting, jerky gestures, or other sudden movements such as suddenly thrusting the upper body forward in the seat as if to leap at the salesperson, finger-wagging, mock karate chops, or quickly placing the hands on the hips with the legs spread farther apart than before.

• Arms crossed over the chest with fingers wrapped in a death grip around the upper arms (another self-control gesture).

• Impatient, forceful finger-tapping or tapping of a pen or pencil.

• Aggressively playing with objects, such as bending and unbending a paper clip or repeatedly stretching and releasing a rubber band.

• Taut facial expression showing defiance, seriousness, or annoyance. No smiling or supportive nodding, tightening of jaw muscles with chin thrust out, and frowns, sometimes accompanied by squinting or sideways glances.

Responding to Negative Signals

—Before you can reduce someone's anger, resentment, or frustration, you must find out the reason behind that person's feelings. Show your sincere concern to get to the root of the emotional situation by asking the person to confide in you. Use strong empathetic listening. If the prospect seems to be holding something back, stop what you're saying or doing and find out what's troubling him.

—Use open body positions and sit back in your chair in a relaxed, nonthreatening fashion. Don't unconsciously mirror the prospect's closed body position or aggressive gestures; use slow and easy body movements.

—Use a calm, soothing tone of voice, a moderate to slow speech rate, and a lower-than-normal volume level to get the prospect to relax.

—Never inflame your prospect further by arguing, vehemently denying something, or going head-to-head on issues temporarily stalled in negotiations. Even if you're right, nothing will be accomplished if the prospect is still upset. If appropriate, show your prospect that you're willing to concede or compromise in certain areas and diplomatically point out that you would appreciate the same sense of fairness and reason from him. Stress points of agreement between you and your prospect instead of dwelling on disagreements.

—If your prospect seems to be frustrated because he is confused about a point that you're discussing, pause momentarily and ask the prospect if he feels that you didn't present something properly. Put the blame on yourself (it's painless) as this example shows: "Ms. Prospect, I must apologize. I get the feeling that I may be going over this set of sales terms and conditions much too fast for you. Because I'm so used to them, I sometimes forget that others are hearing them for the first time. Shall we back up a bit and go over some points, then proceed at a more moderate pace?"

—If the prospect is annoyed about something unrelated to you and your sales call, listen empathetically. If you let him unburden himself on you, he will greatly appreciate your concern, kindness, and sensitivity. If you encourage the prospect to open up and he does not want to talk, tactfully suggest getting together at another time when the prospect can participate in a sales dialogue more productively.

Giveaway Signals:
Deception, Evasion, Lying

Telltale body language is said to be a reasonably accurate barometer of whether a person is withholding something or giving out misleading information. A prospect may falsely tell you that he has no money available to purchase your product or that he is getting a better deal from your competitors. Sometimes a prospect may try to negotiate himself into a better sales situation by feigning apathy about your product when he is actually very interested.

The fact is that people don't always say what they think. Unfortunately, sometimes prospects feel that they must be devious with a salesperson because they perceive many salespeople as being devious themselves. Whether we call it a little white lie, an exaggeration, a fib, or putting someone on, most of us do it regularly to some degree, and we usually rationalize it.

A word of caution is in order here. Especially in this section, I don't want to mislead you into believing that nonverbal communication is a surefire way to detect falsehoods. Even sophisticated lie-detecting machines can be fooled by guilty people who can control their reactions very effectively and by innocent people whose nervousness causes incorrect readings. However, many human behavioral experts believe that lying creates within most people some sort of internal stress that may be caused by guilt, shame, or the fear of being caught and punished or even humiliated. This pressure is bottled up and surfaces in the form of body language gestures. People who are good at being devious will typically control their facial expressions fairly well (a poker face), but other body mannerisms such as those that follow may indicate that they are not telling the truth.

- Squirming in the seat (the "hot seat" syndrome), especially if the person thinks he has been caught lying.
- Frequent lip-licking or wiping lips unnecessarily with a handkerchief or hand.
- Wringing of hands, often exhibited when being pressed to answer.
- Nervous mannerisms that show discomfort, such as finger-tapping, picking at nails, adjusting necktie several times, playing with jewelry, or other nonpurposeful tension-relieving actions.
- Touching oneself more often than usual, perhaps with protective, self-comforting gestures.
- Any sudden, seemingly nonpurposeful body movement at the time of the lie, such as abrupt hand gestures, crossing or uncrossing legs, or leg swinging. Some body language researchers say that the "double cross" (when a person crosses, uncrosses, and then crosses his legs again in the other direction quickly) is a relatively accurate sign that a person feels very uncomfortable with the other person's question or comment, or feels dissatisfaction with a response he has just made.
- Eye contact that goes to one extreme or another: either abruptly looking at the ceiling, floor, or desk, or over-compensating with unnaturally strong eye contact as if to

try to prove he can look you in the eye. This firm eye contact may also be accompanied by nodding in an attempt to reinforce a sense of resolve.

● Voice changes such as higher pitch, higher volume, short and breathy responses, or increased speech rate, as if to force the point. Unnecessary repetition. Unusually long pauses before answering a question may indicate attempts to fabricate answers, and the answers may be short, choppy, and hastily put together.

Responding to Giveaway Signals

—Never imply to the prospect that you think he is lying or directly challenge his statement. Pushing him against the wall will only make him defensive, forcing him to defend his statement in order not to lose face, thus hurting or destroying the rapport between you.

—Sprinkle in several related, but differently phrased, questions designed to check for inconsistencies in your prospect. No third degree tactics, though!

—Analyze whether previously given information (perhaps from others in his company or based on your experience) backs up what the prospect has said.

—If you think your prospect is giving you insincere objections or seemingly unreasonable requests, gently qualify him if it's appropriate. For example, if the prospect tells you that he's interested but thinks your price is too high, you might ask him a qualifying question such as, "Mr. Prospect, you've mentioned that our price is too high and this is preventing you from investing in our product. If we could work out a reasonable price structure for you, would you seriously consider going with us right away?"

6

Effective Questioning

Questions can and should be used throughout each phase of the sales process. The intended goal of any type of sale should initially be to probe and listen, thus giving the prospect an opportunity to participate actively in the selling/buying process. The problem is that too many salespeople are constantly in a talk mode, doing a majority of the talking while expecting the prospect to sit back, listen passively, and somehow see the light. Try using questions as often as possible to force yourself to get the prospect's opinions, which are of paramount importance.

Questions can be effectively used in all of the following parts of the sales cycle: telephone prospecting and getting appointments; approaching the prospect for the first time; qualifying the prospect; getting to know the company and department that you're selling to; discussing features and benefits; giving demonstrations or sales presentations; handling objections, concerns, doubts, misunderstandings, and unrealistic expectations; negotiating terms and conditions of a sales contract; and closing the sale.

You'll see many examples of actual questions to use throughout the sales cycle in chapter 7. But what are the benefits of effective questioning?

1. Questions give you vital information about the sale.
2. Questions help build rapport and develop trust between you and your prospect.
3. Questions enable you to control the sales call effectively.
4. Questions minimize harmful misunderstandings that can occur.
5. Questions reduce resistance to the sale.

Benefit #1:
Questioning Yields Vital Information

A prudent question is one-half of wisdom.

FRANCIS BACON

How many times have you heard someone say, "What you don't know won't hurt you"? That may be true in some situations, but it's a deadly philosophy in a selling situation. As I've mentioned previously, knowledge is power. The more you know about your prospect's company, personal motives, business needs, problems, and goals, and about your competition, the more likely you are to get the sale. Master the art of questioning and you can master the art of selling. Effective probing and listening will enable you to get the critical information you need to qualify the prospect, plan your next sales call, and produce a dynamic, persuasive, and winning presentation. You'll be able to use questions and their answers as the solid foundation to bring you more and faster sales, thus increasing your sales productivity.

Essentially, there are two ways that you can decide which of the prospect's problems and needs can be helped and met through your product or service. The first way is to make a perceptive, perhaps astute assumption based on your own opinions or experiences, or perhaps pieced together from some sketchy, general information extracted from the prospect. The other way—the *best* way—is to ask for information you need from the prospect. It's a short road to disaster for the salesperson who assumes he or she understands. It's infinitely better to hear the actual words from the prospect's mouth and clearly understand his or her attitude and emotions. Getting the right information and the proper amount of it instead of launching into a premature sales presentation is something that professional salespeople feel strongly about, as evidenced by this philosophy that we should all adapt and strictly adhere to:

> "I will never attempt to give a sales presentation to my prospect until I have accurately and completely determined the needs, problems, goals, personal wants, and motivations that my product can help him fulfill. Until then, I will ask questions to find out all the facts, feelings, and circumstances that will later enable me to show my prospect why my product solution is not just a good one, but the *best* one available."

Benefit #2:
Questioning Builds Rapport and Trust

Asking questions of a prospect puts him at the center of attention and shows that you care enough to want to learn more about him and the particular problems and needs that are on his mind. A prospect feels very complimented and appreciative when a salesperson doesn't barge in like a charging bull and launch into a full-blown sales presentation right off the bat. Concentrating on the prospect by questioning and listening rather than talking gives him a feeling of importance. I don't think any of us resents being asked about our thoughts and feelings on a topic and then being listened to carefully. We feel needed, wanted, and respected when others seek us out for advice and ask us questions about topics that are important to us. Prospects consider a salesperson who uses questions properly and then listens intently a smart operator. After all, look whose opinion he asked for!

Asking appropriate questions is a superb way to help establish and maintain warm rapport with your prospect. When a prospect first meets a salesperson, he generally couldn't care less about the salesperson's opinions and ideas or about hearing mere details about his company and product. The prospect's major motive is to find out how that salesperson can help him. Therefore, a prospect greatly appreciates a salesperson who immediately concentrates on him by asking questions about things that will ultimately benefit him.

Make a rule for yourself: except when you are giving a formal sales presentation, never talk more than half of the time during a sales call. Your goal is to get your prospect deeply involved in the selling process. Get him talking. Get him to cooperate. Actively encourage him to participate in a productive, two-way conversation that will benefit both you and your prospect. Make him feel that he has a stake in the buying process. Studies have shown that the more the prospect is involved in a sales meeting, the greater the chance is that he will ultimately buy. The old saying "If they [the prospects] don't share, they won't care" is very true. Asking questions and then effectively listening will clearly and positively set you apart from other salespeople. It enables you to be prospect-oriented and greatly shows your caring and cooperative nature.

Benefit #3:
Questioning Gives You Control
of the Sales Call

As a salesperson, you should set specific objectives that you want to meet by the end of your sales call. Some sales call objectives may be to get another appointment with the prospect in order to continue the sales process, to get the prospect to watch a demonstration of your product or use it on a trial basis, or to actually close the sale, thus getting an order for your product or service. In most first sales calls on the prospect, the primary objectives are to establish personal rapport and credibility, qualify the prospect to determine if he can and will eventually buy your product, and arouse the prospect's interest in your product and company.

Now, in order to reach your sales call objectives, you have to control the details of the discussion and the overall direction of the meeting. This does not mean that the salesperson should try to dominate the discussion, hold the prospect in check, or abruptly and aggressively regulate what happens during the meeting. Since it is the salesperson's clear responsibility to manage the call and take the lead, he must achieve control and leadership in one of two ways. He can talk frequently, thus holding the prospect in check and restraining the prospect's desire to get a word in edgewise—in essence, repressing the prospect's participation. Or he can encourage and draw the prospect into the sales discussion by asking pertinent questions and listening to the prospect's answers, thus motivating the prospect to participate fully in the sales meeting and decision-making process in a way that will help the salesperson meet his objectives.

Have you ever been surprised at how comfortably you can talk with certain salespeople and how easily you agree to buy something from them? They were low-key and considerate, yet they appeared interested and alert. You felt that they were helpful; they assisted you but were not pushy. During the sales process you might have clearly gotten the impression that you were in charge, that you were controlling the situation, because you were talking and taking the lead and the salesperson was listening and supposedly following. If the salesperson was a professional, you were wrong: the fact is *he* was leading and *you* were following, and you probably never even suspected it. That's because the salesperson asked you several pertinent, artful questions and then effectively listened, thus guiding you smoothly and gently (yet directly) to a sale that seemed natural to you. You probably never thought about resisting, hesitating, or bringing up objections because you never felt pressured by the salesperson. You didn't feel you *had* to buy something, but you wanted to. You felt that you had options to exercise. It's amazing how proper questioning and listening can make a prospect naturally feel that he is in complete control, yet the salesperson really directs what is happening in a subtle and socially acceptable way that makes the person a buyer, not just another person being "sold." Even if someone can be sold, he often resents what he feels is a strong manipulative effort on the part of the salesperson.

Here's an interesting story that highlights how a quick, effective sale can be made. The late Fred Herman, a renowned sales trainer, was a guest on "The Mike Douglas Show." Douglas introduced Herman as "the greatest salesman in the world." According to Herman what happened next was not discussed or planned; he had no idea what to expect.

Douglas asked him, "Fred, since you're hailed as the number one salesman in the world, sell me something." Herman began with the question, "Mike, what would you want me to sell you?"—allegedly turning control over to his "prospect." Surprised that a salesman would start off asking something rather than telling, i.e., going into a sales pitch, Douglas looked around and replied, "Well, sell me this ashtray." Continuing with another seemingly innocent question, Herman asked, "Why would you want to buy that?" Douglas, again surprised, looked at the ashtray and replied, "Well, it's new and shapely. Also, it's colorful. And besides, we're in a new studio and don't want it to burn down." Herman had gotten Douglas to mention the fact that he needed and liked the ashtray, not by giving a presentation on it, but by asking a question, getting Douglas himself to say the right words. Herman's next question was, "How much would you pay for the ashtray, Mike?" Douglas, who apparently was stymied, replied, "Well, I haven't bought an ashtray lately, but this one is attractive and large, so I guess I'd pay $18 or $20." Hearing that, Herman immediately closed the sale by saying, "Well, Mike, I'll let you have the ashtray for $18."

This is an example of a quick, complete sale made solely by asking questions, listening, and responding appropriately. The prospect felt in control, but the salesperson controlled. Granted, this example with its off-the-cuff tone might not apply to many types of real-life selling situations. But it proves the point that questioning and listening can be more powerful than telling and launching into a premature sales presentation. Remember, telling ain't selling!

Questioning and listening can give the prospect the warm, secure feeling of taking an active part in the sale—of feeling in control and not feeling as though he is being sold something. Questions can help crystallize the prospect's thinking and steer him to form his own conclusions, rather than telling him what is and what isn't. Using benefit statements in the form of questions can get him to convince himself, producing a cooperative, productive communications climate. Questions can lead the prospect into areas of discussion that you want to focus on while showing the prospect that you appreciate his ideas and opinions.

Questions can also get the prospect off tangents and help him to refocus on what the real issues are. Questions demand attention. Ask the prospect a question, and he is forced to stop what he's doing or thinking and focus on your request.

Benefit #4:
Questioning Reduces Misunderstandings

How often have you misunderstood what your prospect has said or requested? And how many times has your prospect misunderstood something you mentioned or asked for? For most salespeople, misunderstandings occur too often, resulting in frustration, hurt feelings, missed deadlines, loss of respect and trust, and sometimes even cancelled orders.

Asking questions can greatly help to minimize misunderstandings. We've got to listen carefully and constantly remind ourselves not to assume anything. We can't take something for granted based on our definitions, ideas, experiences, values, or knowledge. Using questions to determine if your prospect has fully understood you and using feedback questions to make sure that you have understood your prospect will help to ensure good communication that will translate into sales with minimal problems. Questions are excellent devices to clarify something said and to ensure that all parties involved in the sale understand each other's requests, expectations, and requirements.

Benefit #5:
Questioning Reduces Sales Resistance

As you know, in the sales environment, prospects often have questions, concerns, reservations, or outright objections to something about your product or service, company, or another factor related to the sale. And unless you, as a salesperson, adequately address the prospect's indifference or resistance to buying, you won't get the sale. By using good questioning and listening techniques, we can get the prospect to tell us exactly why he is hesitating to buy and what the extent of his concern is. Once the prospect openly voices some concerns, the salesperson then knows the specific source of potential resistance and can attempt to deal with it.

The most frustrating situations are those where the salesperson thinks everything is going smoothly toward the sale, only to discover later that the prospect is "playing along," hiding some objection that is preventing him from buying. When a prospect is sincerely asked what his feelings are and is listened to nonjudgmentally, he often feels relieved, which makes the problem-solving process easier. A prospect will greatly appreciate your asking tactful questions in an effort to resolve any concerns or problems that are holding back the sale. Unfortunately, some salespeople spout slick, canned answers to beat down the assumed objection the second the prospect alludes to it. Hear your prospect out fully first. Give him every opportunity to express what is really on his mind. In that way, you'll be better able to answer a concern that you have correctly identified, rather than shooting from the hip.

Types of Questions

Questions are excellent tools to use in the sales process. Like any tool, you use each one for a particular job. It's important for you to understand what types of questions to use and when to use them. There are six major categories of questions: open, closed, direct, indirect, leading, and non-leading. By understanding the unique characteristics of each category, you'll be better able to pick the most effective type of questions that will help you reach your objectives.

Open Questions

All types of questions fall somewhere between open and closed (also frequently called open-ended and closed-ended questions). An open question is called by that name because it does not restrict the prospect's response but lets him assume the initiative and carry the conversation where he likes; it's general in nature. Open questions are designed to give a prospect free rein, thus leaving him room to express his full opinions and feelings any way he chooses. So they can elicit a lot of information from the prospect. As an example of how an open question can give a person broad latitude in answering, consider the ultimate open question used by some personnel interviewers: "Could you tell me about yourself?" This question can be answered in any number of ways and is so open that a good talker could spend days—maybe weeks—answering it.

Another example of open questions stimulating conversation is asking someone why something happened. If the person knows why, he can't just give you a one-word answer. Notice how the following examples of open questions used by a salesperson would require a prospect to talk at length in order to answer.

> "What are your major concerns when it comes to meeting your goals of reducing corporate expenses by 12 percent?"
> "How do you feel you could improve your research operations in the next year?"
> "Why do you think your industry is moving in that direction?"
> "What do you believe the reasons were for selecting their products over ours?"

Use open questions when you first meet your prospect. You want to establish quick rapport with him, get him off the defensive, and begin a productive discussion. Open questions make a prospect feel important, intelligent, and respected, because his thoughts and feelings are being solicited, listened to, and valued by the salesperson. The use of such unlimiting questions strongly implies that you respect your prospect's judgment and trust him to select information that is pertinent to the discussion. Also, in doing a majority of the talking, the prospect feels in control, as opposed to how he would feel listening to a salesperson giving a canned sales pitch. Open questions are beneficial for the salesperson because they provide lots of information; they also take the pressure off him because he doesn't constantly have to think of clever things to say or concentrate on a lot of closed questions that must be asked one right after the other. Successful salespeople carefully choose good open questions, then sit back, relax, and take in the discussion. When you need time to think in a meeting with your prospect, ask an open question, listen to the key points being made, and then use the remainder of the time while the prospect is speaking to think of other questions, a response, or a plan of action.

Open-ended probes typically start out with the words *what, why,* and *how* (see Illustration 12 for examples). Responses to such questions will be more lengthy and detailed than a simple yes or no or a terse reply. Another way to get the prospect to open up is to ask the prospect to explain or expand upon what was said, or to make requests such as these (notice the key words):

> "Mr. Prospect, could you *explain* a bit more about how the engineering group arrived at its conclusion?"
>
> "*I'd like to hear more* about your feelings on the turnaround in that situation."
>
> "*Tell me about* what you see as the next logical step we should take."
>
> "Ms. Prospect, *could you go over that again,* but this time, tell me how you think it should have been handled?"

Another way of getting the prospect to continue to open up and expand on what has been said is to use the phrases "What about...?" and "How about...?" For example, "What about extra reliability?" "How about the

ILLUSTRATION 12
EXAMPLES OF OPEN QUESTIONS

"WHY...

do you feel our product can help you now?"

is that, in your opinion?"

do you feel you need the more powerful model?"

is the project being delayed?"

the change in attitude?"

do you believe that happened?"

was he named head of this project?"

are they even considering that risky approach?"

don't other companies follow your lead in this market?"

should you feel that it won't happen again?"

"WHAT...

has been your experience with these problems?"

do you think about the trend toward heavy automation?"

do you think your management would say to that?"

do you feel the answer is?"

happened then?"

will occur if they like our approach?"

can I do to help you solve that problem?"

will it take to convince them?"

does the rest of your staff say about it?"

do you recommend?"

"HOW ...

do you think we
ought to
proceed?"

do you plan to
reach that goal?"

do you compare
our solution to
that of other
vendors?"

can we best
satisfy your
requirements?

will you select
the vendor for
this project?"

do you keep
track of that
information?"

is that possible?"

can I get that
information?"

do you expect to
solve that
problem?"

can I best clarify
the misconception
they have?"

extra savings you would get by installing our communications equipment?" Simply saying "Oh?" or "Hmm?" in a curious, nonjudgmental way can also get your prospect to talk further on the topic.

Although there are many advantages to using open-ended probes, there are also drawbacks. Because they are broad in scope, open questions can enable a prospect to go off on a tangent, talking about areas totally unrelated to the subject at hand. A verbose prospect may go into too much detail on the topic when the salesperson only needs a concise overview. In these cases, a salesperson will have to refocus the prospect's attention repeatedly. With open questions, the salesperson also has less control over the prospect's response than he does when using more focused, closed-type probes. Expect to spend more time in the sales meeting when using open questions frequently.

Closed Questions

Closed or closed-ended questions are so called because they are designed to call for specific and short answers, usually yes, no, or some other brief response. Salespeople use these types of questions when they need to get exact or detailed information and when they want to control the direction and length of the discussion. Using closed questions is an excellent way to clarify and confirm something.

Closed questions can be very useful, but they should be used with caution. They should not be frequently used by a salesperson who is visiting a prospect for the first time. Numerous closed questions can give the impression that the salesperson is interrogating the prospect. If exaggerated use is made of these questions, a prospect may feel manipulated, subservient, frustrated, or angry, and the conversation will have an abrupt, choppy quality. Also, the prospect may get the feeling that the salesperson is not really interested in a full expression of his views, but merely wants brief answers to questions that probably have been fabricated in advance of the meeting, maybe even in rigid checklist form, and are most likely used with all prospects like a telephone survey. Being asked repeated limited-scope questions may make prospects feel that the salesperson is underestimating them or failing to make good use of all the information they can offer.

Closed questions typically begin with the words *do, have, is, can, when, where, will, are, who, am,* and *would.* Here are some examples of closed questions that are intended to elicit a yes, no, or short answer.

> "Is Sally Burns the person to speak to?"
> "How many will you need initially?"
> "What is the latest date I can get back to you on this?"
> "When will the budget be created for this equipment purchase?"
> "Would I be able to have a copy of your project specifications before I leave today?"
> "Will you and Ms. Tyler be able to make it for the next meeting?"
> "Where should the information be sent?"
> "When would you like to see a demonstration?"
> "How many offices do you presently have throughout the country?"
> "Do you typically lease or purchase?"

Closed questions are very effective in confirming something the prospect said earlier, such as "Mr. Prospect, then you feel that.... Is that correct?" or "What you're really saying is that.... Am I right?" In addition, closed questions are good when you have to exert more control over the questioning because time is running short or you need very specific information.

There are degrees of open and closed questions, with

many questions falling somewhere in the middle of the wide spectrum that ranges from very restrictive closed questions to thought-provoking, highly open-ended probes. These in-between questions are designed to elicit replies that are neither brief nor lengthy. Following are some examples of questions from a salesperson that would in most cases elicit moderate-length replies.

> "Is service an important consideration for you?"
>
> "Do you feel strongly about dealing with a large company?"
>
> "Do you think it would be beneficial for you if we could get quicker delivery—let's say one month sooner?"
>
> "Have you spoken to John Richardson about his thoughts on this concept?"
>
> "Would you recommend that we set up a second meeting with your technical staff as the next step?"

A very effective category of in-between questions for a salesperson to use is list questions. These are essentially structured questions that combine the advantages of both open and closed probes. They can give a salesperson a good overview of information while helping to restrict the reply to prevent a prospect from going off on a tangent. These probes, which give the big picture first, enable a salesperson to determine what areas are important enough to ask about next. It's often advisable to explain to the prospect why you are asking structured (more control-oriented) questions. Here are some examples to consider using.

> "Without getting into too much detail yet, could you please list the features that would describe the ideal product for this purpose?"
>
> "I'd like to get a good understanding of what's important to you when selecting a vendor. If it's OK with you, I'd like to ask this question: In priority order, what requirements would you consider necessary for a vendor to have in order to do business with you?"

"Mr. Prospect, I'd like to understand the overall picture first and then get further details later, if that's OK with you. If you had to summarize in order of importance the most pressing problems caused by your present equipment, what would they be?"

Direct and Indirect Questions

The next two categories of question types are direct and indirect questions. It's important to know when to use direct, straightforward, no-nonsense questions and when to use *indirect*, oblique, roundabout questions. If you have already established a comfortable relationship with your prospect and are asking questions about topics that are not private or controversial, you can be more direct in your line of questioning. The following are some examples of direct questions.

"How many items do you have in your inventory?"

"When will you be ordering the machines?"

"Why do you think your present equipment breaks down so often?"

"What were the total sales revenues of your company last year?"

"Who is responsible for controlling this?"

"How much money is being wasted per month because of production slowdowns?"

"Why exactly do you feel that way?"

"Does your company have the cash reserves to invest right now in this type of system?"

Direct questions get right to the point. They are efficient and appropriate when you need straightforward information that you feel the prospect would be willing to give. The stronger the rapport you have established with your prospect, the more direct your line of questioning can be. However, when you are meeting a prospect for the first time or dealing with a defensive person, it's advisable to start off with more indirect questions until the prospect feels more comfortable with you. Also, indirect questions are more gentle and tactful. They can help a salesperson save face and recover more easily if his well-intentioned question inadvertently strays into an area considered confidential, personal, or otherwise off-limits by the prospect. Direct questions in areas that the prospect considers personal are considered unwarranted invasions of privacy and inappropriately aggressive.

There are four basic ways to effectively use indirect questions: the "if we knew" technique, the base of reference technique, the ballpark figure technique, and the third-party technique.

1. *The "if we knew" technique.* This technique involves a part-question, part-statement request for information. It is a way of asking for information that is softer than coming out and bluntly asking for it, because it gives the prospect the option of answering it or casually passing over it. When using this indirect form of request, the salesperson typically explains or justifies why he is looking for an answer, as these examples illustrate.

> "If we knew what your present unit manufacturing costs are, we could estimate roughly how much our new assembly machine can save you."

> "If we knew how much money you had budgeted for this project, we could tell you the size of the computer and the number of terminals we could provide for you."

> "If we knew how much your present machine breakdowns are costing you per month, we'd be able to provide you with a more accurate cost justification based on installing our advanced-technology robots."

2. *The base of reference technique.* This is another indirect way of getting the prospect to give you an answer. In this technique, you provide the prospect with a base of reference—information that he understands and can compare with his situation, thus giving you an answer. This technique is a subtle way of getting your prospect to

respond to you when he has been reluctant to answer direct questions. Here are some examples.

"Mr. Prospect, our automated teller machine can process up to 1000 banking transactions an hour. I'm wondering if your volume requires this high rate."

"Ms. Prospect, a total product package to handle all your needs would run you about $26,000. Is that about how much you had in mind?" (This could also be an indirect way of finding out how much money the company plans to spend.)

Prospects in general are often reluctant to disclose their problems when they first meet a salesperson. A carefully phrased question that suggests that his problems are not unique but are actually shared by many other competent companies can be very effective. Consider the following example.

"A majority of my customers have been experiencing the same types of problems: rising production costs, increased material waste, and problems with cheaper foreign-produced goods. I'm wondering if you're experiencing the same problems."

3. *The ballpark figure technique.* Sometimes prospects are reluctant to give specific information such as exact figures because they consider it confidential or private information or think that giving the salesperson such information could negatively affect negotiations for better terms and conditions on a sales agreement. One questioning technique that enables a salesperson to get an approximate answer is to ask the prospect for ballpark figures, rough estimates, or a range of figures. Here are a few examples.

"Mr. Prospect, is it reasonable to assume that you'd be willing to spend somewhere between $150,000 and $200,000 if you could justify the investment?"

"I know exact figures may be hard to come by, but could you make a rough guess as to how much your inventory shortages are costing you per year?"

"I don't know what your profit margins are, Ms. Prospect, but I would assume they're somewhere in the area of 10-15 percent like the rest of the industry. Is that a fair approximation on my part?"

"I'm wondering if the reject rate for production of your integrated circuits is somewhere around 5 or 10 percent, or is it a bit higher or lower than that?"

4. *The third-party technique.* A very effective questioning technique that may uncover a prospect's true opinions and feelings on a subject is to ask a seemingly innocent question that refers to a third party. It has the advantage of not pitting the salesperson's ego against the prospect's. The third party could be another prospect in the same business, a recognized expert in that business, an article in a respected newspaper or trade publication, or a general reference about a group of unknown people. In this technique, you state the third party's view, then ask the prospect if he agrees or disagrees. This is an excellent way to draw the prospect out without the fear of the two of you personally disagreeing, thus hurting rapport. This indirect questioning technique can find the prospect's "hot" buttons or test his reactions to potentially controversial ideas. There are two steps involved in this questioning technique. First, make a statement revolving around a third party.

"Mr. Prospect, many of my customers [group of unknown people] feel that paperwork costs are getting out of hand today."

"Recently I read in *Office Administration Monthly* that many companies are increasing their use of temporary help during seasonally heavy demands rather than hiring permanent personnel."

"Sarah Redding, who has done extensive study in that area, feels that this is a risky approach because it hasn't been fully tested yet."

Then ask the prospect's opinions and feelings regarding the third party's statement.

"Do you feel that way about it?"

"Do you find that situation to be true in your operation?"

"What are your specific feelings on their comments?"

If the prospect disagrees, at least he is not disagreeing with *you*. Use this questioning technique when asking questions in sensitive areas or to get the prospect to open up without fear of contradicting your ideas or opinions.

One word of caution, though, in using this technique. The name of a person known to your prospect can prejudice the question and give an emotional bias to the answer, depending upon whether your prospect respects and likes the individual mentioned. "Do you agree with the president that...?" is one way of loading a question positively or negatively, depending upon a person's party affiliation and personal feeling toward the president. "Do you agree with the communist principle that states that the way to increase productivity is...?" is slanted to draw a good percentage of "no" answers. If your goal is to elicit an open, honest answer, either make your third-party source general ("people," "some of my customers") or use names of people whom the prospect is not emotionally connected with, either favorably or unfavorably.

Leading and Non-leading Questions

The final categories of questions are leading and non-leading questions. A non-leading question is a question that is phrased in a neutral, unbiased way so as not to put pressure on the prospect to answer it one way or the other. As such, the prospect does not feel obliged to give the answer that the salesperson is specifically looking for. A leading question differs in that it is carefully phrased and designed to influence a prospect strongly to answer a question in the implied direction that the salesperson wants to go. A leading question, then, suggests the answer that is desired by the questioner. Strongly worded leading questions are considered by many people to be manipulative. Depending upon the phrasing of the question, it can vary from mildly persuasive in a positive sense to obviously and strongly biased in a negative sense. If used properly, though, a good leading question can help direct a person toward or away from a certain topic. In a selling situation, leading questions can put a prospect in the right frame of mind by getting him to agree with information that will lead closer to the sale.

Here is an everyday example that illustrates the difference between leading and non-leading questions. A woman whose husband is trim and fit asks a non-leading question about dessert, such as "Honey, would you like another piece of pie?" This question has no implied meaning or judgment attached. The husband is psychologically free to respond yes or no. On the other hand, a woman who is very concerned about her husband's quickly escalating weight anticipates his request for another helping of pie and pre-empts it by asking in a sharp tone of voice a leading question such as "You really don't need another piece of pie, do you?" Or, stronger yet, she asks, "You've had quite a bit to eat already, so I assume you don't want to make a pig out of yourself by having another piece of pie, do you?" Obviously, these questions are designed to discourage the husband from replying yes.

Leading questions are sometimes used by lawyers and news reporters to try to intimidate their witnesses or interview subjects. Asking slanted questions such as "You really don't expect us to believe that, do you?" or "You don't expect our viewing audience to accept that answer, do you?" can automatically put the person answering on the defensive, even if he is fortunate enough to come up with a valid and well-thought-out answer. Many lawyers will often use a leading question that begins with "Isn't it true that...?" or "Isn't it a fact that...?"

Incorrectly used, leading questions that can pull an

answer from your prospect will make him feel manipulated. Even if your prospect answers the way you want him to, he may actually feel the opposite but decide to go along with you to avoid discussion, embarrassment, or loss of your respect. A prospect who is wise to an obviously phrased trick question may go along with the game just to humor the salesperson in order to get rid of him rather than seriously discuss his true opinions. Unfortunately, too many salespeople are taught to use bad leading questions—the obvious, salesy ones that hurt rapport with the prospect and negatively affect the salesperson's professional credibility. Saying to a prospect, "Our product can save you time and money. You want to save time and money, don't you?" can smack of unimaginative manipulation at best.

So far, I've illustrated some extreme forms of negative leading questions. However, leading questions can be very helpful in the sales process when used appropriately. Leading questions can help to elicit a positive response from a prospect concerning the salesperson's company, products, or services. They can be used to jog the prospect's memory or confirm something previously said. Good leading questions can reinforce the prospect's positive attitude toward a product's benefits. Finally, they can be used to refocus a person's thinking—to get him off a tangent or mistaken train of thought and back into discussing the real issues important to the sale.

Leading questions contain phrases often called clinchers, tie-downs, or nail-downs because they are designed to get the prospect to commit to the answer that the salesperson wants. As you'll see later, these phrases can be used in the beginning, middle, or end of a complete leading question. Here are some typical clinchers used in leading questions.

"Don't you feel (agree, think, believe)"

"Aren't they (you, we)"

"Isn't that the case; Isn't that right"

"Wouldn't it"

"Didn't we; Don't we"

"Doesn't it"

"Can't you"

Before we get to examples of some good leading questions to use, let's take a look at some guidelines to consider to make the most effective use of leading questions.

• Phrase your leading questions in a way that's not intimidating, obvious, or manipulative. You want to influence your prospects positively, not maneuver them into a corner by clever logic and wording.

• Be fairly sure that the answer you want from your prospect will come naturally; that is, he will respond freely and openly in the desired way without being coerced.

• Vary your use of clincher phrases. Use combinations of them to avoid obvious repetition that will annoy people.

• Don't use a lot of leading questions over a short period of time. Stay away from several back-to-back leading questions. Even if they are gently phrased, they could make the prospect feel obligated to agree with you constantly.

• Consider using some leading questions in a rhetorical sense, asking a sensible question but not expecting an answer from the prospect. For example, "Of course everyone in your business is concerned about minimizing production costs, right?" The salesperson then continues with "That's why my company has been so successful with clients who are intent on minimizing those costs." However, when asking leading questions that you want the prospect to answer, pause after asking your question to indicate to the prospect that you do in fact want to hear his answer.

• It's especially important to ask leading questions in a natural, friendly, conversational way. Leading questions have more potential than other types of questions to be interpreted as psychologically directed.

Here are some examples of different types of leading questions to use in various portions of the sales process. Notice the phrasing in these questions: a prospect should respond positively to them. Also note that the clincher phrases are alternately used in the beginning, middle, and end of the complete question.

> "That's kind of a nice design touch, *wouldn't you agree?*"
>
> "*Doesn't* having that feature on our drilling press make it much easier for your machinists to use?"
>
> "I clearly understand your concern about price. I would imagine, though, that dealing with a reputable company is equally important to you, *isn't it?*"
>
> "You're right. Price is always an important consideration. But *shouldn't we* take a look at the real issue, which is how much value you will receive from the investment in our product?"
>
> "Based upon all the alternatives that we've looked at, *doesn't* this approach seem to be the most effective?"
>
> "You're perhaps wondering why we decided to use advanced-technology alloy metal in our product's chassis when others use steel, *aren't you?*"
>
> "We're both in agreement that we're heading in the right direction, *aren't we?*"

General Rules for Using Questions

Your primary goal during the first several meetings with your prospect is to get a maximum amount of information from him, which you will later use to present your product or service effectively and explain how it will directly benefit him. Also, you want to obtain this information in the shortest possible time to gain an edge over your competitors and make your selling time more productive. To achieve this end, use probing techniques that are purposeful, specific, and inoffensive to your prospect. The art of asking questions consists of creating and maintaining a conducive climate for productive communication. Asking the right questions in the right way and then actively listening and responding will ensure your getting the answers you need or otherwise reaching your intended objectives. What follows is 18 valuable suggestions and guidelines that will help you become effective at using questions.

Explain to your prospect why you are asking questions and how his answers will benefit him. It's important to "position" questions; often a prospect does not understand how your line of questioning affects the buying of a product or service. For example, in many types of selling, especially those involving high-technology or otherwise expensive equipment, it's essential to show how your product or service can help your prospect reach his business goals and help solve problems in his organization. As such, it's necessary to ask questions to understand better how a prospect's organization functions and what its important business objectives are. Here are some examples of how to position your questions—that is, explain why you will be asking questions that at first may not seem to be directly related to buying your product. Notice in these examples what the salesperson says to the prospect to justify asking questions and motivate the prospect to answer them.

"Mr. Prospect, we've installed over 1,000 machines in organizations like yours. They've received a 60 percent productivity increase in some cases and reduced material waste by 80 percent. We think there is an excellent chance your organization can also benefit from installing our machines. Before we come up with savings and productivity estimates like those, I'll need to learn more about your specific operation and the needs and problems you may have. Would it be all right if I asked you some questions to help me familiarize myself with your company and your department?"

"Ms. Prospect, first I'd like to find out what your overall business goals are—increasing revenues or profits, reducing costs, increasing productivity, or whatever. This will help me understand how our assembly robots can directly help you reach goals that are important to you and also help us later to justify the cost of installing the new machines. If you had to list three or four of your most important business goals in priority order, what would they be?"

Probe in a general manner first when asking questions about a prospect's needs, goals, problems, or other requirements. Like putting together a jigsaw puzzle, you want to understand what the big picture looks like and then later use more specific questions to find out greater details about each need, problem, or goal (the individual pieces of the puzzle). Finally, you want to ask questions to understand how the pieces fit together.

There are three suggested steps in this process. First, ask questions about the broad areas that you are interested in—areas where you think your products and services can help. Next, determine the priority needs, goals, or problems (the primary areas of importance) of the prospect. Finally, ask more specific questions that go into greater detail about the important broad topics you've touched on. These deeper probes are used to find out much more information about a prospect's needs, problems, and motivations to buy.

Following these three steps will enable you to get a great deal of relevant information quickly. Good types of questions to use to get an overview are list or summarize questions, such as the examples mentioned earlier in the section on open and closed questions.

Use a person's name when asking questions. People enjoy hearing their names as long as they're not overused. *Not* using a person's name makes a sales meeting very impersonal. How do you feel when the person you're speaking with never uses your name? The benefit of relevant use of a person's name is that it grabs his attention and can help to establish rapport faster.

Even though we work in a casual, informal business environment compared to years ago or compared to more formal business cultures like in Europe, it's still advisable to start off using *Mr.* or *Ms.* with a person's last name rather than risk the possibility of offending someone by being *too* personal. It's a sign of respect. Once your prospect warms up to you, he will ask you to use his first name only.

Ask one question at a time and give the prospect an opportunity to answer it adequately. Asking one question after the other can confuse the prospect, make him feel pressured, and cause him to forget some of your questions. Here's an example of a salesperson asking too many questions at once.

> "Mr. Prospect, I'd like to ask you these questions: How long has your company been in business? What products does it make? Who are your major competitors? What problems have you been experiencing in your industry? What exposure have you had with our products? Are you aware of how our products have helped other companies like yours?"

Don't make a habit of asking questions and then answering them for the prospect. If done repeatedly, this can be annoying or insulting to the person being asked the questions. Give the person every opportunity to think about a question, fully understand and analyze it, and then answer it. Sometimes, however, it may be appropriate and even necessary to suggest an answer or bring forth an idea to see how the prospect feels about it, especially if the question is important and the prospect either appears to be floundering or simply hasn't given much thought to the matter: for example, "In your opinion, do you think the answer might be...?"

Stay away from questions that may be considered too personal or sensitive (i.e., proprietary or confidential). Samuel Johnson, the famous English author of the 18th century, said, "Questioning is not the mode of conversation among gentlemen." This certainly is true if the questions are poorly timed, too direct for the occasion ("Are you in charge of this department?"), or appear to be too nosy. Some companies treat their financial status, product manufacturing specifications, company organization, or future plans almost as sacred information. If that is clearly the impression that a prospect gives you after you ask some "feeler" questions in these areas, back off and explain why you were asking them. Avoid known sore spots. Stay away from personal questions about the prospect's family, residence, income, or other such subjects. Phrase your necessary questions with tact and diplomacy, or ask indirect questions such as "If we knew roughly what you are experiencing in the area of material waste during your cutting operations, we'd be able to give you approximate estimates of actual savings using our advanced milling machines."

Don't ask numerous closed-ended questions that can put the prospect on the defensive and cause him to cut short his answers. Rapid-fire closed-ended questions can give the prospect the impression that he is a witness being interrogated and given the third degree. This is especially true for the first meeting between salesperson and prospect, when these types of questions can hurt rapport. However, there are times when you have to use closed-ended questions to get very specific information quickly that may, for example, relate to the technical specifications of a prospect's project, such as this series of questions concerning the size of a proposed computer.

"Ms. Prospect, if it's OK with you, I'd like to get some specifics on the technical specifications for the machine you envision. How much memory will you need? [Prospect replies.] How much disk storage is sufficient? [Prospect replies.] How many terminals do you require? [Prospect replies.] What speed printer will you need? [Prospect replies.]"

In these types of detail-oriented fact-gathering sessions, the salesperson needs to ask a series of closed-ended questions because he knows exactly the narrow response the prospect needs to give him. Also, the prospect realizes the need for the salesperson to ask these direct questions and request specific and short answers.

Avoid questions that can turn a prospect off. Any question that can make a person feel stupid, anxious, guilty, wrong, angry, or inferior can ruin rapport. The wording of the question and tone of voice determine the underlying meaning. Don't put the prospect on the defensive. Questions that criticize, challenge, or imply that the prospect is lazy, incompetent, or inconsiderate will cause immediate and possibly lasting damage. Put yourself in your prospect's shoes and ask yourself how you would react to your line of questions. If you want your prospect to cooperate with you, always phrase your questions in either a neutral or a friendly way. Here are a few examples (some dramatic) of questions that would negatively affect the prospect.

—"You didn't send in your warranty papers, did you?"
—"It seems as if you haven't given much thought to these problems. Is that the case?"
—"Can you back up what you just said?"
—"Other companies have been concentrating on improving productivity. Why hasn't yours?"
—"Do you honestly believe that you can get that discount from other suppliers?"

Wait until the prospect completely answers your question before going on to the next one. Don't give the prospect the impression that you are rushing him to answer each question. Ask questions in a relaxed, caring way, waiting several seconds after the prospect finishes his answer to begin your next question.

If it's important to you, make sure that you get answers to the questions you put to the prospect. Quite often a prospect will go off on a tangent, answering in a way that is totally unrelated to the question that was asked. Or the prospect may give a vague, general answer when you need specifics. A Yiddish proverb says, "Better to ask ten times than go astray once." When you need to get vital information, ask the same question again in different words or put the blame on yourself for not understanding. Ask follow-up questions that make the prospect delve deeper into the original answer, if need be. Tactfully ask for more facts, explanations, and justifications through examples, definitions, illustrations, statistics, and written reports. Use questions like the following examples to get the prospect back on track or to give the specific information you originally asked for.

> "Mr. Prospect, getting back to the area of _____, what do you think are other possible causes of the problem?"
>
> "Could you please give me a couple of examples of what you actually mean by that?"
>
> "You mentioned before some key information about how your company makes buying decisions. I'm not quite sure that I fully understand it. Could we quickly go over it once more? I've got a few more questions to ask."

Make your questions easy to digest; begin with friendly questions, then ask relevant questions that are easy for the prospect to answer. When meeting a prospect for the first time, it's a good idea to begin some chit-chat to enable both of you to relax and establish a comfortable rapport prior to delving into the hard-core business at hand. One way to do that is to ask friendly, light, conversational-type questions that relate to the prospect and his business but are of a more personal nature than direct questions dealing purely with the sales call. Here are some examples of friendly questions to establish rapport and get the conversation going in the beginning.

> "Ms. Prospect, I'm very impressed with your new corporate headquarters here. How do you like it compared to the previous location?"
>
> "Mr. Prospect, let me congratulate you on your recent promotion. Francine Simpson in accounting told me about it and suggested I get together with you. You must be excited about your new position. What do your new responsibilities and challenges look like?"
>
> "Mr. Prospect, I couldn't help noticing the beautiful golf trophies on your bookcase. Compared to me, you must be quite a golfer."

After asking some friendly, get-acquainted questions when you first meet your prospect, start asking business-oriented questions that you feel the prospect can comfortably answer. However, you don't want to start asking tough questions about his business or its technical aspects as they relate to your product if you think he will have difficulty answering. An English proverb tells us, "A fool may ask more questions in an hour than a wise man can answer in seven years." Not every question deserves an answer, so give your prospect an out in case he doesn't know the answer. You want to help your prospect save face and avoid embarrassment, and he'll greatly appreciate your sensitivity. Here are some examples of statements you can make if your question doesn't seem to be answerable.

> "Mr. Prospect, you can give more thought to that question and we can get back to it later. Let's move on to something else important to the both of us."
>
> "I should have realized that the answer to that question is not readily at *anyone's* reach. Let's not worry about it."
>
> "My apology. I shouldn't have asked that question. Your

expertise is business; mine is computers. That was a technical question that I should be asking of your technical staff. Let's get back to your business goals."

Stay away from flashy, "salesy," manipulative questions with obvious answers that can hurt your credibility. Avoid these types of questions.

"Mr. Prospect, you're interested in making more money, aren't you?" (Who isn't?)

"Are you interested in improving your business?" (No, he wants it to deteriorate.)

"Ms. Prospect, a lot of businesspeople are interested in increasing their market share. Would you like to do that?" (Of course she would.)

These self-answering questions can be insulting to a prospect's intelligence. Even today, some salespeople still feel compelled to ask these rather crude qualifying and trial-close-type questions that make a prospect brace himself and think, "Another sales pitch is coming my way." Instead of the examples above, use smooth qualifying questions that acknowledge the previously stated or common-sense (universal) goals of your prospect, rather than annoying, obvious questions. Here's an example.

"Mr. Prospect, as a businessperson, you're interested in improving your revenues and profits. Our company has successfully worked with firms just like yours to increase their sales through our advertising programs. Over the past year, 42 of our clients have told us that they have increased their sales by an average of 27 percent as a direct result of our advertising campaigns alone. If you felt confident that, after speaking with me, your firm could potentially benefit as much as the others, would you seriously consider using us to do your advertising at some time in the near future?"

When it's important to get a lot of information from your prospect, resist the temptation to launch into a sales presentation about your product. Sometimes a prospect will give you an answer that's encouraging and exciting. He may reveal a pressing problem that can be easily solved by your product or stress an important business need that can be completely fulfilled by your product or service. The natural tendency is to jump in and enthusiastically relate (in minute detail) how your product can help. It's important to realize that until you get all the crucial facts, do not talk in specifics about your product. Your goal is to probe to get the full picture of your prospect's problems, goals, needs, and motivations that can be solved and fulfilled by your product, not to give an extensive sales presentation on some or all aspects of your product. Your sales presentation will be more complete, accurate, and effective when you gather sufficient information to use later to show exactly how your product will best fit each of the prospect's requirements.

When appropriate, however, it's a good idea to use positive, general support statements between questions that indicate to the prospect that you do have a product or service that will likely help him out. These short statements are designed to get the prospect's attention and then maintain his interest. Here are the differences between a sales presentation and support statements.

—Positive support statements can be used after a prospect clearly identifies an individual, specific problem, goal, or need of his that can be adequately addressed by the salesperson's product or service. A full sales presentation is done after you've identified all the important goals of the prospect.

—A salesperson typically does a sales presentation only once. Positive support statements can be used after each product-related need, problem, or goal is discussed by the prospect.

—Sales presentations can be extensive and take

a good amount of time. A support statement can and should be finished in under a minute.

Since support statements used by the salesperson suggest to the prospect that there is a good chance that the salesperson's product can benefit him, these optimistic statements encourage the prospect to continue the sales dialogue and motivate him to give the salesperson a follow-up meeting. The following example illustrates this technique. Notice that these are not specific discussions about a product, but general support statements or claims that will need to be further explained and proved later, either at the same meeting or at subsequent ones.

> *Prospect:* I need a small computer that is very easy to operate.
> *Salesperson:* Mr. Prospect, I'm happy to hear you say that. Our Mini-Mite computer's features are specifically designed for even inexperienced people to use. I'm confident that it will meet your requirement of easy, quick-to-learn operation. I'd be delighted to show you how easy it is to get started in just a while. If it's OK with you, though, I'd like to find out more about your other needs first.

Here are some shorter general examples of support statements to consider using.

> "We definitely have a strong solution for that problem of yours."
> "Our products are designed to do just what you asked for in that area."
> "I feel we're making good progress here. In just a while, after I find out about all your needs in this area, I'd like to tell you about the exciting ways we can work with you."

Remember that lengthy presentations about your product are inappropriate when you first meet your prospect. Your primary objective is to probe for information that will later be used for an effective presentation. However, these support statements can be used between your questions to do a little selling at the same time. You'll find them very useful on the first call and throughout the entire sales process.

Use short, simple questions that are easy for the prospect to understand. At meetings, you've undoubtedly heard people ask a single, complex, long-winded question that goes on and on until everyone loses track of what the question actually was. Strive to make your questions clear, specific, concise, and simple enough for your prospect to comprehend.

Show confidence when asking questions. Ask a question as if you expect (and deserve) an answer. Prospects should be impressed that you care enough to find out about their needs, goals, and desires. Don't ask questions half-heartedly or in some other way that shows doubt, hesitancy, or lack of confidence. Be careful that the volume of your voice doesn't fall off and that your voice doesn't crack or quiver. Maintain direct, yet comfortable eye contact after asking a question.

Carefully plan your questions before each sales call. It's very important for you to set specific objectives that you want your line of questioning to achieve by the end of your sales call. This will give the call a clear direction and make it much more effective while at the same time showing the prospect that you are highly organized, thus enhancing your overall professionalism. Here are some suggestions to help plan your questions.

1. Ask yourself what you are trying to accomplish during the call, and then determine the types of questions that will fulfill your objectives.

2. Prioritize the information that you need according to three levels: information that is critical to get; information that is important to get; and information that is helpful to get. Spend your time

asking questions on critical areas first, then concentrate on important areas and, finally, on the lowest priority areas.

3. Determine what general categories of information you need to get—e.g., qualifying information, technical details, cost justifications, or other types of data.

4. Analyze the level of details you need and plan the detailed second- and third-level probes you'll use. Sometimes you want to get an overview of several areas; other times, you want to concentrate on just one or two things and get as much detail about them as possible.

5. Plan smooth, non-offensive, meaningful, and specific questions to ensure clarity. Know your prospect and couch your questions in easily understood terms. Be especially careful with the wording of questions that must be asked in areas of potential sensitivity to the prospect.

6. Ask intelligent questions that are logically organized, and ask them in an order that shows that you have given serious thought to getting the right information quickly, thus making the sales call as productive as possible. Avoid jumping from area to area in a way that makes the prospect confused about what you really want to know.

7. Consider creating a question checklist for each sales meeting you go to. It shouldn't be a long, handwritten paper that you have to keep looking down at to read your prepared questions word for word. Obviously, that would annoy your prospect, making him feel manipulated and confined in the conversation and possibly damaging your professional credibility as well. Instead, design a one- or two-page planning sheet containing the

major areas you want to discuss. Under each major area, write down shorthand versions of several questions to jog your memory. (Do not read the questions verbatim.) This question checklist will ensure that you organize your thoughts effectively and will enable you to leave the meeting with a lot of useful information.

Do salespeople pay a lot of attention to planning their questions—or their entire sales calls, for that matter? If I was to take an educated guess, I'd estimate that about 35 percent of all salespeople give no thought to or have no understanding of the questions they have to ask a prospect; 45 percent have a general idea of the types of questions to ask; 15 percent have a very good grasp of relevant questions to use; and 5 percent create a well-written checklist of questions designed according to each prospect and each type of sales call. Which category do you think most of the salespeople in *your* company fall into? It's a proven fact that the most successful salespeople carefully plan their sales calls, with organized questioning as an important part of the overall plan.

To get the prospect to open up more, replace the word think *in your questions with the word* feel. When you ask someone how they "feel," they often give you their emotional response, devoid of hidden meanings. Psychologists, psychiatrists, marriage counselors, the clergy, interviewers, and negotiators make rich use of the word *feel* in their questions. Here are some examples for salespeople to use.

"What are your feelings about that?"
"Do you feel comfortable with our solution?"
"I'd like to get your feelings on what the main issues are."
"I want to listen completely to how you feel at this time."

Such questions often encourage a prospect to be more candid and straightforward than he would be if he were asked analytical questions such as "What do you think about it?"

When planning your line of questions, anticipate all possible reactions from the prospect, then carefully plan your responses or the next appropriate question. Prospects can typically respond to a question in one of three ways. They can answer cooperatively, giving you the exact answer you need; be indifferent or vague, requiring you to use more questions to pull an answer gently from them; or react in a defensive, sarcastic, argumentative, or otherwise negative fashion and ask you to explain and justify the reason behind the question.

Let's say you are asking a qualifying question about your competition of a blunt and caustic prospect who has been reluctant to provide any information. You inquire, "Mr. Prospect, have you looked at any vendors besides my company for your project?" The prospect, perhaps imagining that you want to identify competitors in order to disparage them, thus disagreeing with the prospect's choice of contenders, snaps back with, "Yeah, I have, but why do you want to know? You're not afraid of your competition, are you?" If you have anticipated all likely potential responses to your question, you won't be surprised and thus thrown off balance. You'll be better prepared to ask follow-up questions or react professionally to the prospect's response.

Answering the Prospect's Questions

The other side of the coin is when the prospect asks *you* a question and it's your turn to answer. Keep these suggestions in mind to help you answer your prospect's questions.

—Think of all the typical questions that a prospect could

ask about your product or service, your sales contract's terms and conditions, your company, or any other area related to the sales call. Be prepared with your answers.

—Show your prospect that you are open-minded, flexible, and willing to entertain constructive, reasonable questions. Listen carefully to the question and show interest by smiling, nodding, or leaning or moving forward. If appropriate, pause before answering to give the impression of careful thought and consideration.

—When your prospect raises a thought-provoking question, you can answer it yourself if you know the answer, or ask your prospect what *he* thinks about it to get his opinion or give him an opportunity to display his knowledge on the topic.

—If you're giving a formal sales presentation to a group of prospects, tell them how you would prefer to handle their questions: either at the end of your presentation or as they come up during the presentation.

—Repeat or paraphrase the question if necessary to ensure that you understand it. Try to draw the prospect out further, if needed. For example: "Ms. Prospect, let me make sure that I fully understand what you're asking. You want to know if.... Did I understand you correctly?"

—Answer the question fully and clearly, but briefly. Often a yes or no is sufficient.

—Verify with your prospect that you have satisfactorily answered the question. Consider thanking or complimenting the prospect for his question, when appropriate.

—When you have to delay questions for a later answer because you don't have an immediate response, write the questions down to jog your memory and tell the prospect that you will get back to him with an answer as soon as possible. Don't bluff an answer if you don't know it. Admit that you're not sure and that you will get back to the prospect with a definite, accurate answer as soon as you can.

—If it's called for, answer questions about your product's benefits in a strong, positive way. For example, your prospect asks, "Do you think your product can meet my requirements in the area we just talked about?" If the salesperson is fully confident that the product can, he might say something like, "Mr. Prospect, our product has proven itself in over two hundred companies like yours. There is no doubt in my mind that it will not only meet your needs, but exceed them. To prove it, you get a 30-day, no-obligation trial period and a full refund if you're not fully satisfied that it will benefit you."

7

Sample Questions to Use Throughout the Sales Process

During my years of training salespeople, I've found that they greatly appreciated the way I combine theory and selling concepts with tangible, real-life examples to illustrate general ideas. The very extensive list of questions that rounds out this book can be a valuable sales tool. The many varieties of questions, even within the same sales category, are intended to give you a host of questions to choose from.

Please keep in mind that these are *sample* questions, many using specific products as examples for you to use either exactly as given or as models for your own questions. You may look at some of the questions and say to yourself, "I couldn't ask that question the way it is phrased—that's not me" or "That doesn't apply to my selling environment." Each of us has a unique selling style and personality and, therefore, each of us has a unique way of asking questions. From these sample questions, take any ideas or phrases that can improve your questioning techniques. Develop a tool box of your own questions and pick from it, selecting the right sales tool (question) for the job at hand. You'll find that investing the time to develop a complete list of applicable questions and then practicing them to enable you to deliver them accurately and smoothly will reap huge rewards for you.

Qualifying: Needs, Problems, and Goals

One of the major ways of qualifying your prospect is to determine his specific needs, problems, and goals and then determine to what degree your product can help meet his needs, solve his problems, and reach his goals. The better your product can solve his problems as compared to your competitors' products, the better your opportunity to make a sale. Consultative selling techniques are based on a salesperson's ability to identify all of the prospect's needs, goals, and problems that can be helped by the product, find out the importance and priority of each, and finally give an impacting sales presentation that clearly, accurately, and convincingly shows exactly how the product can best meet the needs of the prospect. Therefore, it's imperative to question the prospect fully and find out as much information as you can about situations where your product is a perfect fit.

Sample Questions

Probing for goals, needs, and problems:

> "In order for me to fully explain how our product can uniquely help you, I'll have to learn more about how your department presently operates. Can I ask you a couple of brief questions before I talk about my product and its potential value to you?"
>
> "In the area of assembly, what do you see the new robots actually doing?"
>
> "If you had to list three or four of your major goals in priority order for this project, what would you say they are?"

"What specific areas of your present operation would you like to enhance?"

"Could you tell me a little bit about what you see as your overall needs for a product of this type?"

"You said your needs in this area are.... Have I adequately identified all your needs at this point? Are there any others you feel are important to you at this time that we should discuss?"

"Do you anticipate having any new goals for this project added to the ones you've already mentioned in the future?"

"Are those short-term or long-term goals?"

"Could you please prioritize those four needs [problems, goals, objectives] that you've mentioned to me?"

"How do you feel our products can help you in the area of _____?"

"What are some of the things you'd like to accomplish using a product like ours?"

Probing for problems:

"How do you see that problem impacting the operation of your department?" "How much do you see that problem costing you per month?"

"What types of problems have you been experiencing in your operations?" "How important is it for you to solve those problems?" "When would you like to eliminate those specific problems?"

"What would you say is the major cause of that problem?"

"How can our product help with that problem?"

"Many of my customers who are in a business like yours have been experiencing problems in these areas: _____, _____, and _____. Do you find that in your situation?"

Qualifying: Timing Considerations

Another important aspect of qualifying your prospect is to find out when he intends to buy your product. If your prospect is interested in buying soon, you should spend more of your time with him as opposed to prospects who are interested in buying in the future (maybe 6-12 months from now). You also want to find out other timing aspects concerning your sale such as when your prospect wants to see a demonstration of your product or when delivery is desired. Your object is to separate the window shoppers from the serious buyers.

Sample Questions

"When are you thinking of purchasing this type of product?"

"Have you decided when you will select a particular vendor for this project?"

"Is there any cutoff date by which you have to select a vendor for this project?"

"Are there any particular pressing reasons why this purchase decision has been postponed for two months?"

"When are you looking for a proposal [presentation, demonstration] from the vendors?"

"Is there anything that we can do to speed things up?"

Delivery of your product is another aspect of timing that could be an important consideration influencing a sale.

Probing for delivery time:

"When would you like to get delivery?"

"What do you see as the latest acceptable date for delivery?"

"Would you be willing to accept a partial delivery by _____ and full delivery on or before _____?"

"How important is quick delivery in the vendor selection process?"

Prospects who purchase products or services that require lengthy and complex installation, construction, or assembly such as computers, production machinery, buildings, or aircraft are concerned about getting the products built or installed promptly and properly. A prospect may have already developed an installation or construction schedule that he expects vendors to meet. Beating his schedule and proving to him that your product or service is quicker and easier to install and is less disruptive to his present operations can help sway the sale in your favor.

Probing for installation schedule:

> "Ms. Prospect, do you have a planned date when you would like this equipment up and running in a real production mode?"
>
> "Is there an absolute deadline that the installation has to be completed by? In the unlikely event that that date is delayed because of unforeseen circumstances, what happens?"
>
> "Are you planning the implementation in stages? Could you describe those stages for me and attach beginning and ending dates for each?"
>
> "When you get the installation completed, will you immediately switch over everything from your present operations, or will you begin in a phased approach, transferring operations to your new equipment one stage at a time?"
>
> "How do you see us specifically helping you during the implementation?"
>
> "How soon after delivery would you like to begin the installation?"
>
> "Have you gone through an implementation like this before?" "What were your experiences?" "How long did it take?"

Qualifying: The Approval Process

Qualifying also consists of determining if the person you're dealing with can make a buying decision; that is, does he have the legal authority to sign a purchase agreement or issue a purchase order? If that's not the case, the person may be able to help you convince the real decision-maker to choose your product or service. A major goal in selling is to call high—make an appointment to see the highest-level individual in the organization that you can in order to deal directly with the person who has the real authority to make a purchase decision. While it's a goal to strive for, it's often not possible to get a meeting with a higher-up in the organization. However, it's important to understand who actually can make that decision to buy and then attempt to work with that person. You want to find out what the decision-making process is in your account to try to influence it. It's very important to pinpoint the power brokers who are the real decision-makers and whose opinion will sway the sale.

Sample Questions

"Are you the person who will be making the sole decision, or are other people involved? Who else might be involved in evaluating vendors for this project and what weight does each have in influencing the decision?"

"Ms. Prospect, could you describe for me the actual process involved in making this type of purchase decision?"

"Whose final authorization is needed prior to issuing a purchase order?"

"In this type of approval process, which person or group has more weight in swaying the decision to buy?"

"How active is the person who actually signs the sales contract in the evaluation process to select a vendor?"

"Are there any behind-the-scenes people whom I should be calling on?"

"What chain of command in your organization should I follow in this approval process?"

"How long does this entire approval process usually take?"

"Can I depend upon you to support our product solution to your upper management?"

"Are you using any outside consultants who are involved in helping your company to select a vendor for this project?"

Qualifying: Your Competition

In order to determine if you have a good chance of getting a sale from your prospect, you have to find out about your competition—who they are and how your prospect feels about them relative to your product and your company. If your prospect is presently using your competitor's product, you should find out how the prospect views the pros and cons of the product. Using questions to find out about your competition will not only help to qualify your prospect further, but it will also give you important information to help create a strategy to counter your competitors.

Sample Questions

"Mr. Prospect, would you mind telling me what other vendors you are considering for this purchase?"

"Ms. Prospect, how did you go about selecting those particular companies as possible vendors to deal with?"

"What do you see as the unique strengths and weaknesses of each contending vendor's product?"

"Ms. Prospect, after hearing a little bit about our company and its products, how would you compare us to some of the other companies you're considering for this purchase?"

"Mr. Prospect, you've mentioned that you've been doing business with the XYZ Company for a number of years. What do you both like and dislike about them and their products? What would cause you to consider switching vendors for your next purchase?"

Qualifying: Financial Criteria

Finding out if a prospect can pay for your product and how he intends to pay is another important qualifying step. What good is having a prospect who is eager to buy your product when he might have problems getting money to pay for it?

Sample Questions

"Has this particular project been officially funded yet? Could you share with me approximately how much money is presently available to spend?"

"Is there a *maximum* budget limitation—a ceiling that vendors have to be aware of?"

"I realize that your budget has only $230,000 available for purchase of this equipment. Assume for a moment, however, that a vendor like my company could provide additional benefits such as.... If that were the case, could additional money be approved for a larger budget?"

"What does it take to get money budgeted for a product like ours? Is there any way that we can help you get it budgeted?"

"Are there any time constraints toward spending the money in the budget? For example, if it's not spent within the next two months, is the budgeted money lost until the next quarter or the next year?"

"Our product typically costs between $150,000 and $220,000, depending upon the options you add. Does that price range fall within your purchase guidelines?"

"When do you think money could be budgeted for this project?"

"Is there a certain purchase dollar amount beyond which you would have to get someone else's approval besides your own?"

"Do you typically purchase, lease, or rent this type of equipment? Do you have any specific guidelines related to these that I should be aware of?"

"Do you anticipate any problems obtaining funds if you decide to buy this type of product?"

When purchasing expensive equipment or services, prospects often have to put together a cost justification for the expenditure of funds. Whether it's buying or leasing computers, corporate aircraft, a new plant and equipment, advertising programs, or vehicles, the company has to calculate how the purchase will translate into either short-term or long-term financial benefits. A company's senior management wants to make the best use of the company's money by investing it in buying those products or services that will ultimately give them the greatest return on investment within an acceptable risk level. If you sell a product that typically requires cost justification by both you and the prospect, you must understand how to influence the process and translate your unique product features into financial benefits.

Sample Questions

"Is a cost justification study necessary to get management approval to order this type of product?"

"When will the cost justification actually begin?" "Has the cost justification been done yet?" "What phase is it in right now?" "Could you tell me who might be in charge of it?"

"What departments are involved in the financial study?"

"Was your cost justification based on any one vendor's proposal or was it based on a study of the estimated benefits that would be realized from installing this general type of equipment?"

"Could you share with me the overall findings of your cost justification?"

"Have your top management people seen the cost justification yet? What were their feelings on it?"

"How important is financial justification in the overall process of selecting a vendor? What would happen if a vendor cost 10 [15, 20] percent less or 10 [15, 20] percent more than most other vendors?"

"What specific financial criteria do you use in your cost justification—for example, do you use payback, return on investment, net present value, or internal rate of return?" "What financial measuring technique is the most important? Why?"

"Do you have certain specified limits for each of the financial methods? For example, Mr. Prospect, do you have a minimum payback period or minimum return on investment required for this type of purchase?"

"Could you tell me specifically how your company calculates

payback [or return on investment, etc.]?"

"Could you explain to me the individual elements that are part of each calculation? For example, Ms. Prospect, in your return on investment calculation, you mentioned that savings and profits were used to calculate it. Where do you see the savings and profits specifically coming from? In what areas do you see the greatest savings [or profits]?"

"How do depreciation and investment tax credits fit into your justification?"

"Do you have a copy of your cost justification for us to look at to see if we could exceed your criteria and further add to savings or profits?"

"How do you think we should work with you on your cost justification?"

"Let's say for a moment that we could increase your clerical productivity better than the other vendors you're considering—perhaps by as much as 20 percent. As an approximation, how much of a positive financial impact in your area do you think that would be?"

Qualifying: Selecting a Particular Vendor

It's important to find out a person's or a company's formal buying criteria—how a vendor is selected for a purchase. Besides being another factor in qualifying your prospect, this is important information that may help you influence your prospect's buying decision. Buyers often decide to buy from a particular vendor for reasons in addition to the features or specifications of that vendor's product or service; things like the reputation of your company and previous experiences that your prospect has had with your organization can have a big influence on the sale.

Sample Questions

"Does your organization have any standard criteria that a vendor must meet prior to your buying from that vendor?"

"How familiar are you with our company and its products?"

"What are your feelings about us?"

"Are other people in your company familiar with us? What do they think?"

"Have you ever dealt with us before? In what way?"

"Could you please describe for me the three or four most important considerations that you will be basing your buying decision on?"

"How would you rate us compared with other companies making similar types of products?"

"Could you describe the ideal product you would like to buy and the ideal company you would like to do business with?"

"How will you select a vendor for this project?"

"In your opinion, what do you feel our company has to do to get your business?"

"What are the key things that you're looking for in dealing with a vendor on a long-term basis?"

"What specific things will you be basing your buying decision on?"

"Are there any particular Federal or local codes or regulations that affect your dealings with vendors?"

"What do you consider the best qualities in a vendor?"

Technical or Product Requirements

Whether you're selling sophisticated electronic equipment (computers, communication equipment) or other types of capital equipment (industrial machine tools, assembly equipment, vehicles, lighting products), you're often dealing with prospects who are very knowledgeable about the general features of products like yours. In high-tech or industrial selling situations, you may be dealing with prospects who are technical or engineering-oriented and whose job it is to evaluate different products from several vendors. You should ask questions to determine what features or specifications are required by these product-knowledgeable prospects.

However, please keep in mind that the types of questions that follow are almost never asked of senior-level executives who typically are not interested in discussing your product's design characteristics, specifications, or detailed features. Instead, these executives are more interested in the operational and financial benefits (increased revenues and profits, reduced costs) that result from using your product.

Sample Questions

"What do you see as the most important features in a product of this type?"

"Have you or anyone else developed detailed technical specifications for the machines you will be considering for this important project? Is it in written form and, if so, would it be possible for me to get a copy of it to study back in the office?"

"Have you created, or are you in the process of creating, a request for proposal that will go out to the vendors you're considering for this project?" "Could you tell me what it basically contains?" "Do you have a deadline set for when you expect the vendors to respond to it?"

"If you had to prioritize the most important features that you're looking for in this type of product, what would they be?"

"What special characteristics in a product of this type do you feel would cause you to select one product over another from the various vendors competing for your business?"

"How do you feel our product specifications and features compare to others that you've studied for this project?"

"You mentioned that you need to replace your old machines. What exactly are you looking for when it comes to buying new machines?"

"How would you describe the ideal _____ for your company?"

Your Sales Presentation

An effective sales presentation should specifically focus on the unique needs, problems, and wants of your prospect.

You want to show that there is a perfect fit between what the prospect needs and wants and what your company has to offer. Each prospect may have special needs, or he may have the same types of needs as other prospects like himself but with a different priority and emphasis for each. Because each selling presentation should be tailored to that prospect and his requirements, canned presentations are deadly. Certainly, there may be parts of your presentation that you give to every prospect, but each overall presentation has to focus directly on the unique needs, concerns, and motivating factors ("hot" buttons) of that prospect or group of prospects.

Analyzing your audience completely and accurately is crucial to sales success. Prior to giving a comprehensive sales presentation to your prospect(s), it's a good idea to ask about the type of presentation, the information in it, and other aspects about it that will bring winning results. This is especially true when giving complex team presentations that are time-consuming and costly to develop.

Sample Questions

"What areas of our product and its solution do you feel I should especially focus on during my presentation?"

"Ms. Prospect, considering who will be attending the sales presentation, how technical do you believe my presentation should be?"

"Our presentation team has created a planned agenda for the presentation next week, Mr. Prospect. I'd like to discuss it with you to make sure that it will clearly address the areas of key importance to you. I'd appreciate your recommending any changes or enhancements."

"Mr. Prospect, I feel that I could do a comprehensive job during my presentation if I could schedule an hour and a half with your group. Is that OK with you?"

"Could you tell me how many people will be attending the sales presentation from your department? Would it also be possible to get a list of their names and what their responsibilities on this project are?"

"Mr. Prospect, with this group, do you recommend that we have a separate question and answer period at the end of the sales presentation, or should we open up the presentation for discussion at any time?"

"Ms. Prospect, what do the other people who will be attending the presentation know and feel about my company, its products, and the proposed solution that we've briefly talked about?"

"What types of questions or concerns do you think the group will have regarding our product and its solution?"

"If you and the others in the group feel that we definitely have the best solution to offer among all the other vendors, do you think the group will agree to go ahead and order our equipment?"

"For our presentation, I'll be bringing handouts on.... The information in them will cover.... Do you feel those are totally sufficient, or would you recommend something else?"

"Ms. Prospect, since you know most of the people attending the sales presentation, is there any special strategy or approach that you would recommend with this particular group?"

"Mr. Prospect, I've come up with an initial approach and product solution for your needs. Before I formally present the final version, I'd like to have you review it and tell me if I'm on the right track. Is that acceptable to you?"

Handling Objections

Objections from a prospect are usually dreaded and feared by just about all salespeople, even experienced ones. An objection is anything that is a source of sales resistance, thus preventing the prospect from making a buying decision. It could be something about your product, your company, or your sales terms and conditions that your prospect doesn't like, or something your prospect needs or wants that your product cannot fulfill. A strongly worded (and perhaps very valid) objection can knock a salesperson off guard; a series of objections can wear a salesperson down and cause him to lose confidence in his product or himself. A salesperson should anticipate objections, find out what they are, and manage them efficiently.

A prospect will not go ahead and make a decision to buy until his apprehensions are adequately resolved. That's why it's so important to get the prospect to open up—to tell you what's on his mind. The questions that follow are designed not only to find out what the objections are and why the prospect feels that way, but also to give you ideas on how to respond to them in a question format.

There are two important considerations to keep in mind when handling a prospect's objections. The first is to listen and remain professional. Let the prospect know by your behavior that you're not worried, nervous, annoyed, disappointed, frustrated, apologetic, defensive, or angry about the objection. Act relaxed, friendly, confident, patient, concerned, and open-minded. Secondly, whether asking questions or responding to some form of sales resistance, don't use the word *objection* in your conversations. Call the resistance an *item*, a *comment*, an *area*, a *point*, a *question*, or even a *concern*. Calling something an objection can add a negative tone and extra weight to the prospect's concern and may put him on the defensive.

Sample Questions

"What particular areas of our proposal do you have questions or concerns about?"

"If we can address that item to your complete satisfaction, will you consider going ahead with an order with us?"

"Why do you feel this is a requirement at this time?"

"Is there anything at this time that would cause you to hesitate to go ahead with this investment?"

"What items do you feel we need to discuss and work on further before you can seriously consider making a decision to purchase our product?"

"How do you feel we should resolve this concern of yours?"

"What do you feel our first step should be in resolving this?"

"I was wondering—why do you feel that way?"

"Besides the area of price, are there any other concerns, or is that the only item holding you back from buying?"

"We don't have feature A, which you would like to have, on our product. As you know, though, we do have features B, C, and D, which no other product has. In view of the fact that these unique features will provide such benefits as..., do you feel having feature A is more important than getting all the other benefits that no other product can give?"

"I understand your feelings and comments about this. Before we discuss it, however, are there any other questions or concerns you may have that would prevent you from feeling completely confident that you're making the right decision to buy?"

"Mr. Prospect, I understand your feelings about potential risk, but don't you feel that our comprehensive guarantee with its iron-clad protection plan will give you more than adequate protection?"

"So my understanding is that there are three primary issues we have to resolve before you consider purchasing from us: they are _____ , _____ , and _____ . Is that correct? Are there any other issues that you feel would impact upon your decision to buy?"

"Ms. Prospect, I get the feeling that something is telling you to hold off buying. I've given you all the information on how our products can specifically benefit you, and I have no doubt whatsoever that a decision on your part to purchase will be an excellent one. But it's not what I think that counts; it's what *you* feel that's important. Before I leave this afternoon, I'd like to find out exactly what seems to be troubling you or causing doubts. If we can't resolve it, then you'll feel good about holding off on this purchase. But if we do address the questions you have, you'll know beyond a doubt that buying was the right decision. Either way, I believe discussing it will ease your mind. Could you tell me what it is that's really causing you to hold off?"

"Ms. Prospect, do you feel our price is acceptable? [Prospect responds that price is fine.] How about our overall product performance and reliability? Do they meet all your expectations? [Prospect responds yes.] And what of delivery, installation, and our guarantee policy—are they totally adequate for you? [Again, prospect responds yes.] If all those important areas are to your liking, I guess I'm a little confused as to what might be causing you to delay making this decision."

"Mr. Prospect, you said our price is too much. How much is 'too much' in your opinion?"

"Ms. Prospect, when you say that our price is too high, do you mean that you feel you can get the same type of product for less money, or is it something else regarding the price?"

"You mentioned that our price is higher than you had expected. What did you anticipate for a product of this type?"

"How much money were you thinking of investing in a product like this? [Prospect replies.] If we could reduce our price to nearer that figure, do you think we could do business together?"

"You're absolutely right! Price is always a key factor. It seems expensive. If I were in your shoes, I imagine I would ask myself these questions: Do I need this product? How will it benefit me? Is this the best one to buy out of all my choices? Should I wait or should I buy now? Mr. Prospect, do you feel this way?" (If the prospect says yes, you go on to answer all these questions for him; if no, you ask the prospect what the real concerns are and then address them.)

"This extra feature seems expensive, but look what it gives you and what the overall benefits are. [Salesperson talks about benefits.] Since you'll be using our machine for around three years, this feature breaks down to a cost of about $4.30 per working day. It's your decision. Do you feel it's worth it based on the benefits you'll get from it?"

Another way of eliciting an explanation of a concern by your prospect is to restate the concern in identical or similar language with a rising voice inflection, thus producing a question, and then pause. This will almost force a prospect to explain, expand upon, or justify his concern.

Prospect:	"It's too expensive for me."
Salesperson:	"It's too expensive?"
Prospect:	"Your terms and conditions are too inflexible."
Salesperson:	"You feel they should be more flexible?"

General Trial Closes

Trial closes are valuable questions to ask throughout the sales process to gauge your prospect's reactions to what you are presenting. You want to find out if your prospect agrees with the benefits that your product or service can provide and, most important, how ready he is to make a commitment to buy. Trial closes in essence are sales thermometers that can tell you if the prospect is cold, warm, or burning with desire to get your product. You can begin to use trial closes even on the first sales call you make.

A trial close differs from a close in that a trial close asks for an opinion from the prospect and a close asks for an action—a commitment on the part of the prospect to make a decision to buy. Because people enjoy being asked their opinions, not only do trial closes get the prospect involved in the sale, but they also tell the salesperson how much further selling may be necessary and which tactics will be the most effective in closing the sale. Trial closes are gentle, indirect ways of getting closer to the sale. They ask for feelings, appraisals, opinions, and estimations rather than decisions, which prospects are often reluctant to make easily in the sales process. Salespeople like trial closes because they can use several of them to build up their confidence prior to asking an actual closing question and to determine if the timing of their close is appropriate.

Here are some situations when it would be appropriate to use trial closes.

—After you talk about a major strength of your product or service and how it can specifically benefit your prospect

—After a summary of all your major product benefits

—At any point in the sales cycle to determine what the prospect is thinking and feeling toward your product and company

—After successfully answering an objection, a concern, or a question from the prospect

—After getting a strong buying signal

—When your product demonstration and sales presentation are completed

Sample Questions

"How do all those features appeal to you?"

"How does our proposal compare to the others that you've seen?"

"Do you feel that we're making progress so far?"

"It seems that you can really use our product with its valuable features to improve the operation of your business. What's your feeling on that?"

"Based on the operational benefits we can give you, our price, and our cost justification, how do you feel about our proposal at this point?"

"Overall, what's your impression of our product so far?"

"Based on the positive comments and reactions that I've heard from you, I assume you feel pleased with our presentation. Is that the case?"

"How do you feel about the way our product specifically handles this important requirement of yours?"

"Before we move on to the next area in the presentation, do you ladies and gentlemen believe that we have fully met your needs in this area?"

"Comparing our presentation and its solution to the others you've seen from other vendors, how would you rate ours when you weigh all the pros and cons of each?"

"Ms. Prospect, in your estimation, does this seem like the product to meet all your specifications?"

"Are there any other remaining items to discuss, or do you feel confident that we've addressed all your needs, questions, and concerns?"

"I really love the way our product performs this operation and I think you do, too. Am I correct?"

"Do you think our product is the answer to help solve your problems?"

"Many of my customers who have selected our equipment over others on the market bought it for these reasons: 1._____; 2._____; 3._____; and 4._____. Are those reasons important to you and your situation?"

"Are we in complete agreement with our proposal, or are there remaining areas to focus on?"

"This will provide the cost savings you require, won't it?"

Qualifying Trial Closes

These types of questions combine further qualifying your prospect and trial-closing him at the same time. They usually start with words like *if, assuming,* or *let's say.* Here are some examples that can be used at appropriate times in the sales cycle.

"If we can meet all the goals you've mentioned, do it at a price under $200,000, and give you delivery in four months, do you think we stand a good chance of getting your business?"

"Assuming that you feel we can best handle your needs in the data processing area and that we can meet or exceed your service requirements, all in a way that gives a return on investment of at least 28 percent as you've mentioned, would you recommend going with us as the selected vendor for this project to your management?"

"Let's say that at this point in the process, I feel extremely confident that we can do all the things you've mentioned in a way that's superior to the other vendors you're dealing with. After our presentation, if you and your staff agree that our overall solution is the best one for you, would it seem likely for us to get a purchase order shortly after my presentation?"

"My understanding is that if our equipment outperforms all others as you've mentioned, our price is at least competitive, we can guarantee a shipment of ten machines in a month, and we can install them by September 26th, you will recommend going with us for this project. Do I understand your feelings correctly?"

"What do you feel it would take at this point for you to select us as the vendor and give us a purchase order shortly?"

Finally, there is a category of trial closes that will tell you with perhaps 99 percent accuracy whether your prospect is ready to buy. These trial closes use questions that concern your product specifically. The questions are designed to tell you whether the prospect has already decided and is ready to be closed. They are asked in a way that assumes the prospect has already decided to buy. Obviously, you should ask prior general trial close questions to make fairly sure the prospect is primed and ready. These trial closes will remove any guessing on your part as to whether to close the sale or wait and do more selling.

"Mr. Prospect, your computer should be delivered in about two months. How many of your staff do you think we ought to enroll in our training course that begins in a month?"

"Our warranty policy for our machines will expire in six months from date of purchase. Would you prefer to include on the same ordering form the service charge for the following six months?"

"To go along with your drill presses, will you be ordering a supply of lubricants from us, or do you have another source you use?"

"Should we set up a scheduled installation date right now?"

"Will you be using our shipping insurance, or would you prefer to handle that aspect yourself?"

"What specific date do you want us to make a first delivery to you, and where shall we deliver first?"

"I feel for your requirement that you'll only need our medium-duty model, since you only operate eight hours a day. We could always trade those in to give you our heavy-duty model later if necessary. You'll be saving almost 28 percent. What do you want to go with?"

Notice that no mention of actual buying is made, but a strong, positive answer that indicates that the prospect has already selected your product will give you the confidence to ask a specific closing question.

Closing the Sale

For many salespeople, asking closing questions is psychologically difficult. It's the moment of truth when the prospect will either go along and agree to buy or lease the salesperson's product or turn him down. My strong belief is that closing should be the easiest part of the sale, because if everything else has been done efficiently and correctly up to that point, the prospect should almost close himself. If rapport and credibility have been established with the prospect; if the salesperson has uncovered all the needs, problems, and desires of the prospect with relation to his product; if an excellent sales presentation has been given; and if the salesperson has handled the prospect's objections, questions, and concerns in an effective, professional manner, the close should be an incidental event that merits no dread or fanfare. The close is really nothing more than the natural culmination of the sales process.

Here are some times in the sales cycle when you should consider asking closing questions.

—After you have successfully given a sales presentation outlining all the major benefits of your product or service

—After you've tried a strong trial close on the prospect and he has responded in a positive manner, clearly indicating he is inclined to buy

—After successfully answering any final objection, concern, question, or request for information that the prospect has

—When the prospect has given you strong buying signals (for example, saying, "I absolutely need delivery of your product by the 14th of next month. Can you deliver by then?")

You want your close to be timely, natural, and comfortable. You don't want to jump in for an abrupt, obvious, go-for-the-jugular sales tactic. There is no need for high-pressure tactics that can turn into resentment later, even if the prospect buys and is relatively satisfied. The pressure should come from within the prospect because he is motivated to buy.

When asking closing questions, it's crucial for the salesperson to act relaxed, confident, and nonchalant, as if the prospect has already made up his mind to buy. The salesperson should act secure that his recommendation to the prospect to buy is, beyond a shadow of a doubt, the absolutely correct one. If a salesperson behaves or asks a closing question in a manner that's rushed, harried, nervous, or unsure, the prospect may suspect that something is wrong and that his decision to buy is not the right one, and he may hesitate. If a salesperson is acting pushy, impatient, or otherwise demanding, the prospect may recoil in a defensive manner; the sale, after much hard work, could be lost.

Practice asking closing questions so that they appear smooth, natural, and matter-of-fact. Choose your words carefully, but avoid stuttering, stammering, or otherwise searching for words. Your closing attitude should be as follows: My products and my company are the best, my prospect will definitely benefit by purchasing from me, and I'm going to get this sale. If you develop a positive mental and emotional attitude, closing will come a lot easier.

There is often a fine dividing line between asking a strong trial close question and asking an actual closing question. A closing question is one that specifically asks the prospect to make a buying decision or to act on the salesperson's request (e.g., sign the salesperson's sales agreement or issue a purchase order). A close may also be a statement of action on the part of the salesperson that the prospect has to prevent in order not to buy (for example, the salesperson tells the prospect that he will write the order up "if it's OK" with the prospect. After asking a closing question, do not speak, even if the prospect doesn't quickly answer. Many times your prospect will need some time to think over what he may consider to be an important decision, and interrupting his train of thought could prolong getting the sale or even jeopardize it.

Many books on selling tell the reader to phrase a closing question in such a way as not to give your prospect the chance to say no, because he will do just that if given the opportunity. That sort of old-fashioned thinking still prevails today in spite of the fact that we are dealing with very knowledgeable, sophisticated buyers. Don't be afraid to ask a yes/no closing question; if a prospect is not willing to buy, your clever closing question is not going to push him to do it. Unless a buyer is a spineless jellyfish, he is going to buy what he wants when he wants it and from whomever he wants. The most important types of closing questions are those that are phrased to be perfectly natural. That means that a prospect shouldn't be shocked to hear a salesperson ask for a natural conclusion to the sale and, he hopes, the beginning of a long-term business relationship.

Sample Questions

"Well, it looks as though you've made your mind up. Shall

we go ahead with writing up the order and setting delivery for March 14th, as you've mentioned?"

"I guess the only thing to take care of at this point is the paperwork. I'll need an authorized purchase order endorsed by you. Shall I wait for the purchase order now, or shall I pick it up sometime later today?"

"Are there any other questions you have, or is there anything else you'd like to discuss before we go ahead and write the order up for you?"

"When I write the order up in a moment, what delivery and billing address shall I put down?"

"I know the purchase order has to be approved by several people besides yourself. After you endorse it, when do you think we can have the completed purchase order with all the necessary signatures mailed to us?"

"I've really enjoyed working with you over the last two months, and I look forward to a successful implementation of our equipment in your business. To enable me to get your machines ordered as soon as possible, I'm wondering if it would be convenient to have your secretary type up a purchase order and have you sign it before I leave. I could then hand-deliver it to the purchasing department for their signature. Would this be OK with you?"

"I'd like to get your order in today before our price increase takes effect next week. Is this agreeable to you?"

"Ms. Prospect, our product solution will increase your productivity 30 to 40 percent, improve your manufacturing quality, and reduce overall costs by at least 20 percent. You've agreed that these figures are realistic and even conservative. I'm anxious to help you get started reaching these goals. I recommend that we go ahead with our solution. I'd like to get your approval to do that."

"I'm pleased. It certainly sounds as if we've satisfied all your requirements and questions. If there's nothing else to go over, with your permission, I'd like to go ahead, write the order up, then have you check it over and authorize it. Is that OK with you?"